T0329214

Cambridge Elements ≡

Elements in Religion and Violence
edited by
James R. Lewis
University of Tromsø
Margo Kitts
Hawai'i Pacific University

RELIGIOUS TERRORISM

Heather S. Gregg
U.S. Army War College

CAMBRIDGE
UNIVERSITY PRESS

CAMBRIDGE
UNIVERSITY PRESS

University Printing House, Cambridge CB2 8BS, United Kingdom

One Liberty Plaza, 20th Floor, New York, NY 10006, USA

477 Williamstown Road, Port Melbourne, VIC 3207, Australia

314–321, 3rd Floor, Plot 3, Splendor Forum, Jasola District Centre,
New Delhi – 110025, India

79 Anson Road, #06–04/06, Singapore 079906

Cambridge University Press is part of the University of Cambridge.

It furthers the University's mission by disseminating knowledge in the pursuit of
education, learning, and research at the highest international levels of excellence.

www.cambridge.org
Information on this title: www.cambridge.org/9781108730891
DOI: 10.1017/9781108583992

First published 2020

A catalogue record for this publication is available from the British Library.

ISBN 978-1-108-73089-1 Paperback
ISSN 2397-9496 (online)
ISSN 2514-3786 (print)

Religious Terrorism

Elements in Religion and Violence

DOI: 10.1017/9781108583992
First published online: July 2020

Heather S. Gregg

U.S. Army War College

Author for correspondence: Heather S. Gregg, heather.gregg@armywarcollege.edu

ABSTRACT: How can the world's religions, which propagate peace and love, promote violence and the killing of innocent civilians through terrorist acts? This volume aims to offer insights into this puzzle by providing a brief overview of debates on terrorism, a discussion on religion and the various resources it provides groups engaging in terrorist acts, four arguments for what causes religious terrorism, brief examples of religious terrorism across faith traditions, and a synopsis of deradicalization programs. This discussion shows that, when combined with certain political and social circumstances, religions provide powerful resources for justifying and motivating terrorist acts against civilians.

KEYWORDS: religion; terrorism; extremism; violence; deradicalization; counter-radicalization

ISBNs: 9781108730891 (PB), 9781108583992 (OC)
ISSNs: 2397-9496 (online), 2514-3786 (print)

Contents

1 Introduction

On July 1, 2013, *Time* released an issue of its magazine with the picture of a Buddhist monk on its cover and the caption "the face of Buddhist terror." The monk, Ashin Wirathu, had helped form several Buddhist organizations designed to aggressively confront what he claimed to be efforts by Myanmar's Muslim minority to "Islamize" the country. Wirathu insisted that, despite making up about six percent of the population, Muslims in Myanmar "get money from Muslim countries, and they want to conquer us and destroy Buddhism" (Bookbinder 2013). Through the proliferation of cell phones, the Internet, and social media, these Buddhist organizations spread sermons propagating conspiracies of Muslim designs to "deracinate" the country of its Buddhist population through forced conversions, high rates of childbirth, and marriage to Buddhist women. These narratives sparked several anti-Muslim riots and terrorist acts throughout the country that cost thousands of lives and, at its worst, helped justify a wave of forced migration in 2017, which produced "more than 655,000 [Muslim] refugees" (Amnesty International 2018, 270). How could a Buddhist monk, who adheres to the principle of *ahimsa*, or nonviolence, help foment indiscriminate violence against a minority group within its own country?

Similar examples of religious justifications for acts of terrorism against innocent people can be found elsewhere. For example, white supremacists in the United States, Canada, and Europe draw on a fringe interpretation of Christianity, known as Identity Christianity, to argue that white Anglo-Saxons are the true Israelites, Jews are the anti-Christ, and people of color are the offspring of Satan. Several white supremacist movements and groups have sprung up under the influence of Christian Identity to call for a racial holy war – "RAHOWA" – with the hope that "wars between and among the races will lead to an Aryan victory and restructuring of society that will reinstate the White man to his dominant place on earth and thereby restore 'order'" (Sharpe 2000, 608).

Another example of religion's involvement in indiscriminate acts of violence comes from Japan. On March 20, 1995, a self-proclaimed religious group, Aum Shinrikyo, attempted to release sarin gas in the Tokyo subway, killing twelve and injuring thousands. This attack against innocent civilians was part of a wider strategy to hasten the end of times and bring salvation to its faithful members. Paradoxically, Aum Shinrikyo claimed that it needed to "destroy the world to save it" (Lifton 2000).

More recently, a group calling itself *ad-Dawlah al-Islāmiyah fī 'l-ʿIrāq wa-sh-Shām*, more commonly known as ISIL or ISIS in the West, began slaughtering Shia Muslims, Yazidis, Christians, and secular Sunni Muslims by the thousands in Syria and Iraq. Its call for mass bloodshed quickly spread around the globe, and in 2014, its spokesperson, Abu Mohammed al-Adnani, ordered:

> If you can kill a disbelieving American or European – especially the spiteful and filthy French – or an Australian, or a Canadian, or any other disbeliever from the disbelievers waging war, including the citizens of the countries that entered into a coalition against the Islamic State, then rely upon Allah, and kill him in any manner or way, however it may be. ... Smash his head with a rock, or slaughter him with a knife, or run him over with your car, or throw him down from a high place, or choke him, or poison him. (Bayoumy 2014)

How could the world's religions, which propagate peace and love, become entangled in terrorist acts designed to terrify and kill innocent civilians? Academics and policy makers have struggled to answer this question and make sense of groups carrying out these incidents, their motives, and how religion has shaped their behavior, if at all. A surge of literature has produced a wide array of explanations for the emergence of groups like al-Qaeda and ISIL, ranging from those who consider both the definition of religion and its involvement in violence a Western construct and a "myth" (Cavanaugh 2009) to those that claim that certain religions, Islam in particular, are inherently violent and at the root of these acts of terrorism, what is known as "essentialist terrorism" (Ali Khan 2006).

Still other scholars have pointed out that terrorism done in the name of faith is not new; it stretches far back in history and is not confined to just one religious tradition. David Rapoport (1983) and Walter Laqueur (1987), for example, note that religiously motivated terrorism can be found as far back as Second Temple Era Judaism, when Zealots – a radical group within Judaism – assassinated Roman officials, with the aim of compelling their withdrawal from the region. In India, Hindu Thuggs strangled unsuspecting sojourners as a sacrifice to the goddess Kali. And Shia Muslim "assassins" killed innocent civilians as part of a secret religious fraternity. In Christianity, the rise and fall of Crusading, which spanned several centuries beginning in the eleventh century CE, included both church-sanctioned efforts to push back Muslim advances as well as groups that formed outside the jurisdiction of the church and that perpetrated indiscriminate acts of violence against civilians, including Muslim, Jewish communities and eastern Christians (Gregg 2014b).

These wide-ranging debates over what defines religiously motivated terrorism, or if it exists at all, are further challenged by rigorous debates over what terrorism is, in and of itself, and whether or not it should be considered a distinct form of violence. This perennial debate has produced at least 109 definitions of terrorism by one count, confounding what terrorism is and how to counter it (Hoffman 1998). Religiously motivated violence and extremism suffer from the same lack of consensus. Terrorism scholar Peter Neumann (2013, 873) argues that debates over the term radicalization, which many assert leads to religious terrorism, not only have failed to produce a consensus on its meaning but have led some scholars to "claim that radicalization is a 'myth' promoted by the media and security agencies for the purpose of [anchoring] news agendas ... [and legitimizing] policy responses." These debates, in other words, are still trying to produce a consensus on what religious terrorism is, what causes it, and how is it countered.

This volume aims to offer some clarity on these debates. It begins by providing a very brief introduction to literature on terrorism in Section 2. Drawing from key scholars across academic disciplines, it includes debates surrounding terrorism's targets, methods, actors, and intended effects, focusing specifically on terrorism as threats or acts of violence that intentionally target civilians, as opposed to military or government targets.

Section 3 begins to unravel the seemingly contradictory possibility that the world's religions could be a source of violence and terrorism against civilians. It proposes that religions are about much more than propagating peace, love, and ethical conduct. Instead, they are complex systems of resources, including scriptures, stories, doctrine, networks of practitioners, seasoned leaders, and even material resources like money, buildings, printing presses, and so on that, under certain conditions, can be useful tools for justifying, motivating, and perpetrating acts of terrorism. Religion's unique contribution to groups wanting to challenge the status quo is that it has this array of readymade tools that can be used to facilitate terrorism.

Section 4 builds on this discussion to consider the conditions under which groups use religious resources to justify and perpetrate acts of violence against civilians. It presents four broad causes of religious terrorism in particular: fundamentalist calls for purity both within the faith and within territory believed to be essential to the religion, religious nationalists' aim to seize the state and impose religious rule, efforts to hasten the apocalypse, and the conditions under which individuals are radicalized and take up these calls for violence. These causes of religious terrorism underscore the contexts in which groups call for terrorist acts in the name of faith and the religious resources they use to justify and perpetrate these acts.

Section 5 provides examples of groups that have engaged in acts of terrorism on behalf of their faith. Specifically, it describes the rise of Salafi Jihadism, the birth of ISIL, and the conditions under which it has justified brutal acts of violence against civilians, including fellow Muslims. It then provides a brief overview of the rise of Identity Christianity, the white supremacist movement in the United States, and its use of Christian scriptures and resources to justify violence against civilians. This section also describes the rise of militant strains of Buddhism in Myanmar and the creation of the 969 Movement and Ma-Ba-Tha, organizations of Buddhist monks using faith to justify cleansing the country of Muslims. It then considers the conditions under which American Rabbi Meir Kahane founded the Jewish Defense League in 1968 and its call for violence against what it believed to be enemies of Judaism in the United States and Israel, culminating with the 1994 murder of twenty-nine Muslims in prayer at the Tomb of the Patriarchs in Hebron. Finally, the section looks at an example of a "New Religious Movement" – Aum Shinrikyo – and its use of several faith traditions to justify attacking Japanese civilians with a weapon of mass destruction (WMD) in 1995.

Section 6 concludes with a discussion of efforts aimed at countering religious violence and terrorism, including deradicalization programs that target individuals incarcerated for acts of religious terrorism, counter-radical efforts aimed at addressing vulnerable populations, and anti-radicalization – community-based approaches designed to prevent radicalization from taking hold in wider populations.

This discussion aims to show that religiously motivated terrorism is not a new phenomenon, nor is it confined to one faith tradition. Moreover, religious terrorism may be on the rise, given the problematic combination of factors that make it more likely, including war and other forms of trauma, perceived moral corruption of society and government, and the foreign policies of other countries believed to be unjust. These factors, when combined with key resources from within the faith, including charismatic leaders, their interpretation of scriptures and beliefs, the use of key religious resources, and the camaraderie, purpose, and a sense of identity that radical groups provide may increase the likelihood of religious terrorism. Finally, access to more lethal weapons, including WMD, could make religiously terrorism more deadly.

Ultimately, countering religious terrorism requires governments to do more than bolster homeland security or execute counterterrorism missions aimed at disabling terrorist organizations; these actions do not address root causes. Rather, governments and communities need to work at the local level to address the factors that make certain individuals and groups vulnerable to embracing violence and terrorism in the name of faith and to address and undermine the interpretations of faith systems calling for violence. Communities around the world have begun to tackle these problems through various deradicalization, counter-radicalization, and anti-radicalization programs, and provide clues for how best to counter religious terrorism.

2 What Is – and Is Not – Terrorism

Any investigation of religious terrorism needs to begin with defining what terrorism is and what it is not. However, this is not an easy task, and most discussions on terrorism tend to struggle with providing a basic, agreed-upon definition of the phenomenon. Walter Laqueur (1987, 11), for example, notes that the term "has been used in so many different senses as to become almost meaningless, covering almost any, and not necessarily political, acts of violence." Bruce Hoffman (1998, 37–39) identifies 109 different definitions of terrorism and specific words used to describe the phenomenon. Hoffman further points out that the US government cannot even agree on a common understanding of terrorism, and the State Department, the Federal Bureau of Investigation (FBI), and the Department of Defense all have different definitions. Despite the lack of consensus, reviewing debates on terrorism will help inform a discussion on how religion may affect this type of violence.

Many definitions of terrorism focus specifically on the target of terrorist acts, namely civilians. For example, Walter Laqueur (1987, 72) defines terrorism as "the illegitimate use of force to achieve a political objective by targeting innocent people." This definition notes the deliberate targeting of civilians or "innocents," through either the use or threat of violence, to affect their attitudes and behavior. Louise Richardson (2006, 4) offers a similar definition: "Terrorism simply means deliberately and violently targeting civilians for political purposes." She goes on to assert that "if the primary tactic of an organization is deliberately to target civilians, it deserves to be called a terrorist group, irrespective of the political context in which it operates or the legitimacy of the goals it seeks to achieve" (2006, 6). However, focusing specifically on the targeting of civilians when defining terrorism throws into question groups that target militaries as a means of advancing their goals. For example, Hezbollah's 1993 suicide bombing of the US Marine Corps Barracks in Beirut – which killed 306 people, including 241 military personnel – may not fall within the parameters of targeting just civilians. Similarly, the 1996 al-Qaeda attack on the Khobar Towers in Saudi Arabia, which killed nineteen US service members, was not an attack on civilians, nor was the 2000 attack on the USS *Cole* off the coast of Yemen. Therefore, defining terrorism exclusively as targeting civilians leaves out important examples of violence that many would identify as terrorism.

Other definitions focus on the act to define terrorism, as opposed to the goals. As such, terrorism is a tactic – a means to greater ends. Tore Bjørgo (2005, 2), for example, defines terrorism as "a set of methods or strategies of combat rather than an identifiable ideology or movement, and involves premeditated use of violence against (primarily) non-combatants in order to achieve a psychological effect of fear on others than the immediate targets." Similarly, Richardson (2006, 6) asserts, "It is the means employed and not the ends pursued, nor the political context in which a group operates, that determines whether or not a group is a terrorist group." However, focusing only on the act of violence would include the many examples of mass shootings in the United States, such as the October 2017 Las Vegas mass shooting, which killed fifty-eight people and was the single largest mass shooting in US history. The gunman had no known motive for the act. Within this definition, attacks like this and the many other school shootings in recent US history would be no different from acts driven by greater political motives, such as the 2014 San Bernardino shooting, which killed fourteen, and the 2016 Pulse Nightclub massacre, which killed forty-nine. Both of these attacks were carried out by individuals claiming allegiance to the ISIL.

Other definitions of terrorism focus on identifying the type of actors engaging in terrorist actions. Several scholars of modern terrorism, for example, tend to focus on nonstate actors as the perpetrators of terrorist acts, distinguishing these individuals and groups from governments (Richardson 2006; Hoffman 1998). For example, Kydd and Walter (2006, 52) define terrorism as "the use of violence against civilians by nonstate actors to attain political goals." However, groups that use terrorism often also receive support from governments, what is typically called "state sponsorship of terrorism." Still other states use nonstate actors as "proxies" or a deniable foreign-policy arm of a country's government to pursue various goals. Hoffman (1998, 27) describes this as "warfare whereby weaker states could confront larger, more powerful rivals without the risk of retribution." For example, the Lebanese-based Shia group Hezbollah has received considerable training and support from the state of Iran (Ranstorp 1997). More recently, Hezbollah fighters have appeared in conflicts backed by Iran, such as the fight against ISIL in Syria and Iraq, and in the civil war in Yemen (Ali 2019). Therefore, the line between nonstate actors that use terrorism and government support of these groups is difficult to discern.

Still others focus on the goal of terrorism. Hoffman (1998, 14), for example, notes that terrorism is "fundamentally and inherently political ... and ineluctably about power: the pursuit of power, the acquisition of power and the use of power to achieve political change." He thus defines terrorism as "violence – or, equally important, the threat of violence – used and directed in pursuit of, or in service of a political aim" (1998, 15). Similarly, Martha Crenshaw (Sick 1990, 53) defines terrorism as "the deliberate and systematic use or threat of violence to coerce changes in political behavior. It involves symbolic acts of violence, intended to communicate a political message to watching audiences."

Considerable scholarship has focused also on the ideological motivations of terrorism. For example, Gregg (2014a) differentiates terrorism of the "left" (anarchist and Marxist inspired), terrorism of the "right" (racist, nationalist, and fascist motivations), and "ethnic separatist" terrorism, which aims to achieve autonomy from a country or military occupation. David Rapoport (2004) argues that terrorism has gone through four distinct "waves" in the modern era, beginning with anarchism, then "anti-colonial," followed by the "new left" (communist-inspired terrorism), and the current wave, which is religious terrorism. Rapoport notes that each of these waves lasted around forty years (or about a generation). Similarly, Walter Laqueur (1999) argues that terrorism has had different motivations and that the rise of fanaticism, which he defines as an ideology of mass destruction, could combine with new technology, notably WMD, to cause catastrophic terrorism. Laqueur identifies extreme interpretations of religion, and particularly the concept of the apocalypse, as a potential driver of catastrophic terrorism.

Furthermore, several different academic disciplines investigate terrorism, producing distinct results based on these intellectual approaches. Political scientists, for example, tend to focus on the ways in which terrorism challenges governments or other sources of political power (Hoffman 1998), how terrorism is used as a strategy that "signals" commitment to governments and populations about certain intended goals (Kydd and Walter 2006), and how rational actor models can explain the conditions under which groups employ terrorism (Anderton and Carter 2005). Sociologists and anthropologists look at the ways in which certain social and cultural circumstances produce and support terrorism or reject it (Killcullen 2009; Atran 2010). Psychologists consider the conditions under which individuals join and engage in terrorist acts, and whether or not they have mental pathologies (Crenshaw 2006, Horgan 2009, McCauly and Moskalenko 2017). And religious scholars look at the ways in which religious resources, such as sacred texts, symbols, and networks of adherents, are used to motivate and justify acts of violence (Juergensmeyer 2000; Gregg 2018). Each of these approaches produces a slightly different focus on the definition and causes of terrorism.

The government and international agencies responsible for fighting terrorism have also produced differing definitions of terrorism that echo debates about the actors, targets, means, and purpose of terrorism. Reuven Young (2006) notes that differing legal definitions of terrorism hamper both international and domestic efforts to counter this threat. For example, as the agency responsible for investigating and prosecuting criminal acts in the United States, the FBI (2018) distinguishes between international terrorism, which it defines as "perpetrated by individuals and/or groups inspired by or associated with designated foreign terrorist organizations or nations (state-sponsored)," and domestic terrorism, which is "perpetrated by individuals and/or groups inspired by or associated with primarily U.S.-based movements that espouse extremist ideologies of a political, religious, social, racial, or environmental nature." The North Atlantic Treaty Organization (2017, 114) defines terrorism as "the unlawful use or threatened use of force or violence, instilling fear and terror, against individuals or property in an attempt to coerce or intimidate governments or societies, or to gain control over a population, to achieve political, religious or ideological objectives." These definitions do not suggest a consensus on the definition but rather include a mixture of actors (individuals, groups, countries), motives (ideological, racial), targets (individuals, property), and goals (coerce governments or societies).

Finally, several scholars note that terrorism is an inherently negative term. Hoffman (1998, 30), for example, observes that "the terrorist . . . will *never* acknowledge that he is a terrorist and moreover will go to great lengths to evade and obscure any such inference or connection." Hoffman cites Jenkins, who notes that "use of the term implies a moral judgement; and if one party can successfully attach the label *terrorist* to its opponent, then it has indirectly persuaded others to adopt its moral viewpoint" (1998, 31). Richardson (2006) cites Osama Bin Laden and Abimael Guzman of the Shining Path, who both point to state actions as the true terrorism and their own actions as justified in the name of political liberation. Therefore, terrorists will rarely, if ever, self-identify as such, which complicates an understanding of the phenomenon.

Conclusion

From this broad debate on terrorism, the following discussion will pay particular attention to acts or threats of violence that deliberately target civilians. It will aim to shed light on how groups, usually nonstate actors, claim to act on behalf of a faith tradition and use religious resources to justify, motivate, and execute terrorist acts against civilians. It will consider the wider social and political circumstances that give rise to these groups and the various goals for which they are fighting. And, finally, it will offer thoughts on how to counter this threat.

3 Religion and Terrorism

How can the world's religions, which propagate peace and love, promote violence and the killing of innocent civilians through terrorist acts? Answering this question requires, first, discussing what religion is. As will be described, religions are about much more than propagating peace, love, and ethical conduct. Rather, religions are complex systems of scriptures, stories, doctrines, and laws, along with social and material resources that, under certain conditions, can be useful tools for justifying, motivating, and perpetrating violence, including terrorism. Religion's unique contribution to groups wanting to challenge the status quo is that it has this unique array of readymade tools that can be used to facilitate terrorism. This section outlines three broad sets of religious resources in particular: scriptures, stories, and beliefs, which leaders can interpret to justify and motivate terrorism; social resources, including leaders and social networks; and material resources, such as money and physical infrastructure. As will be described in the following sections, these resources, when combined with social and political circumstances, help facilitate violent acts that deliberately target civilians in the name of faith.

What Is Religion?

Similar to debates on what terrorism is and is not, there is no agreed-upon definition of religion or even if there is such a thing as religion. Anthropologist Talal Asad (1993), for example, argues that the very concept of religion is a Western construct, borne out of colonialism and anthropological studies, that creates a false dichotomy between secularism and religion. Theologian William Cavanaugh (2009) builds on this discussion to argue that religious violence, like the broader definition of religion, is primarily a Western concept that builds upon and perpetuates religion as distinct from liberalism and other modern ideologies and, by extension, the way in which it causes violence. Recognizing the importance of this debate and the role that Western constructs and biases play in explaining the causes of religious violence and terrorism, this discussion will nevertheless attempt to broadly explain what religion is and how it can perpetuate violence against civilians.

Typically, definitions of religion rely on the presence of a god, gods, deity, or transcendent power. For example, the *Cambridge English Dictionary* (2019) defines religion as "the belief and worship of a god or gods, or any such system of belief and worship." Similarly, the *Oxford English Dictionary* (2019) defines religion as "the belief in and worship of a superhuman controlling power, especially a personal God or gods." However, these rather narrow definitions leave out a number of critical elements that are found in most faith traditions.

Broader definitions of religion include a system of beliefs that also involves specific acts, like prayer, rituals, and sacrifice. For example, Sociologist Max Weber (1963, 28) defines religion as "the relationship of men [*sic*] to supernatural forces which takes the forms of prayer, sacrifice and worship." More comprehensive definitions include not only a faith system but also a community of practitioners, religion's experiential aspects, and the resources that religious groups tend to have. Religious scholar Ninian Smart (1996), for example, proposes that religions are complex worldviews that have seven dimensions: doctrine or philosophy, rituals, myths or narratives, experiences and emotions, ethics and law, social aspects, and material resources. Echoing Asad and Cavanaugh, Smart is quick to include Marxism and nationalism as religions under this broad definition.

These comprehensive definitions stress that religions are much more than just a belief in a god, or even ethical conduct, and better capture the array of resources that could be used to justify and promote violent action, including terrorism. Specifically, as will be discussed in the following subsection, religions' scriptures, doctrines, beliefs, myths, and narratives make up the raw material that leaders can use to form ideology or complex narratives that provide "a set of beliefs for how the world ought to be, a critique of how the world currently is, and a course of action for realizing that world" (Gregg 2010, 293). Religions also have considerable social and material resources that are useful tools for mobilizing and perpetrating terrorism. Each of these types of resources, and how they can help perpetuate terrorism, are explained further as follows.

Scriptures, Beliefs, and Ideology

Most of the world's religions contain a mixture of scriptures, stories, laws (formal and informal), and doctrines (codified beliefs) that explain the origins and history of the world, the purpose of life, and righteous conduct of the faithful. Within these sources that explain the faith, most religious traditions have narratives that depict epic battles of good versus evil, supernatural violence, and human aggression, including stories of persecution against faith traditions and violence carried out in defense or promotion of the faith. Some scholars argue that the presence of these scriptures and stories forms the basis of religiously motivated violence. For example, sociologist Mark Juergensmeyer (1992) notes the importance of religions' scriptures and stories as a source of violent behavior. Specifically, he proposes that epic battles between forces of good and evil, stories of conflict or persecution, and battles for survival of the faith are common in most of the world's religious traditions:

> Whole books of the Hebrew Bible are devoted to the military exploits of great kings, their contests relayed in gory detail. The New Testament does not take up the battle cry immediately, but the later history of the Church does, supplying a Christian record of bloody crusades and religious wars. In India, warfare is part of the grandeur of mythology. The great epics, the Ramayana and the Mahabharata, are seemingly unending takes of conflict and military intrigue. (1992, 107)

Juergensmeyer goes on to note that in the Buddhist majority country of Sri Lanka, "Sinhalese legendary history as recorded in the Pali Chronicles, the *Dipavamsa* and *Mahavamsa* – which have assumed almost canonical status in Sri Lankan society – amounts to a triumphal record of great battles waged by legendary Buddhist kings" (1992, 107). Similarly, Sikhism has narratives that tell of persecution by Muslim Mughal emperors during the early days of the faith. And Islam has scripture that justifies the use of force under specific circumstances, including the often sited "Sword Verse" (Sura 9:5): "But when the forbidden months are past, then fight and slay the Pagans wherever ye find them, and seize them, beleaguer them, and lie in wait for them in every stratagem (of war); but if they repent, and establish regular prayers and practice regular charity, then open the way for them: for Allah is Oft-forgiving, Most Merciful."

As will be described in the following sections, these scriptures and stories, including those of great battles and violence, which are well known to practitioners of the faith, can be powerful resources for justifying the call for violence in the name of faith. However, scriptures and stories by themselves are not the cause of violence, but rather it is specific interpretations of scriptures and stories calling for violence that are significant. These interpretations are the product of individuals, usually leaders, who are shaped by the social and political circumstances in which they live. As will be described, specific interpretations, the leaders that created them, the social and political circumstances in which they were derived, and the support they receive from individuals and communities help explain the conditions under which religion becomes involved in terrorism.

In addition to scripture, several key beliefs, which may or may not be present in scripture, can be useful resources for justifying and motivating violence. For example, most of the world's religious traditions purport that this world will end at some point and that a new world or era of peace and prosperity will emerge in its place. For many religions, the end of times will culminate with an epic battle between good and evil, where people will suffer and their faith tried but, ultimately, will usher in a new period of justice and peace. For example, Christianity has expectations of the apocalypse and a period where the dead will be brought back to life, people will be judged, the righteous will be rewarded, and the wicked will be condemned. Islam, like Christianity, has the expectation of the Final Judgment preceded by a series of battles. Even Hinduism has the expectation of the end of times with the arrival of Kalki, the tenth avatar of Vishnu. In many cases, the end of times is announced by signs that the end is near, "and that the faithful must rise up, stand firm in the face of trials and hardship, and defend the faith" (Gregg, 2016, 11). As will be described further in Section 4, under certain circumstances, the faithful's anticipation of the apocalypse can help foster the belief that committing mass atrocities and bloodshed will hasten the end of times and usher in a new era of eternal salvation marked by peace and justice.

Another belief in many religions that, under certain circumstances, can be used to justify violence is the distinction between the "chosen" – the idea that certain people are special to or called by God – and the "others," which is everyone else. Gabriel Almond, R. Scott Appleby, and Emanuel Sivan (2002), for example, observe that a heightened sense of "elect membership" and the desire to create "distinct boundaries" between the saved and the damned are symptoms of groups turning toward extremism. This tendency to separate the "chosen" from the "other" can turn violent when paired with the perceived need to purify the "unclean" from within the faith or wider society. Furthermore, the notion of "chosenness" paired with a claim to specific territory can elevate the possibility of believers turning to violence to cleanse the land of those outside the faith. This particular understanding of "us" versus "them," under certain circumstances, can cause one group to dehumanize the "other" and help motivate indiscriminate violence against these civilians, as the cases in section 5 will demonstrate.

Martyrdom is yet another key belief in many religions that can be a useful tool for motivating terrorism. Martyrs are individuals who die, often suffering in the process, in defense of their faith (Cook 2007, 1). The concept of martyrs exists in virtually all of the world's religious traditions. For example, Second Temple Era Judaism experienced an episode of martyrdom during the Maccabean revolts of 167–160 BCE, in which thousands of Jews chose death over allowing the Hellenization of Jewish society (Bickerman 1947). Martyrs in Christianity date back to the very origins of the faith, when Stephen was dragged outside the gates of Jerusalem and stoned to death by Jews after proclaiming Jesus the messiah. The concept of martyrs also exists in Sikhism, where the fifth leader (Guru) was killed by the Mughal Emperor Jahanjir after refusing to convert to Islam and the ninth leader was killed by Emperor Aurengzeb in defense of the faith (Syan 2012). During World War II, Japan used a particular interpretation of Buddhism mixed with Shintoism to create the kamikaze ("wind of god") attack units, which promised salvation to pilots and other troops that engaged in suicide tactics against the enemy (Axel and Kase 2002). And martyrdom is an important cornerstone of Islam; it is mentioned specifically in the Qur'an and the faith has several distinct types of martyrs, including those who die when actively fighting for their faith and in battle, but also those who die as part of a plague or illness and women who die in childbirth (Cook 2007).

Another key belief in most of the world's religious traditions that can, under certain circumstances, be used to motivate violence and terrorism is the concept of salvation. Broadly defined, salvation is saving, purifying, or liberating people from the forces of evil and (re)uniting them with the good (Gregg 2014b). Importantly, two salvations exist in most religious traditions: eternal salvation and earthly salvation. For example, most understandings of the Abrahamic faiths (Judaism, Christianity, and Islam) believe that eternal salvation is promised to the faithful after this life, usually described as "heaven," or "paradise," and that those who turn against God will be damned, or go to hell. In Buddhism and Hinduism, eternal salvation occurs through the release from reincarnation (*moksha*) into a state that transcends this cycle, which is *nirvana*. This release from the cycle of life, death, and rebirth is attained through knowledge, enlightenment, or by doing good deeds or performing one's duty to caste in Hinduism (Conz 1963, Biarradeu 1989). As will be discussed in the following sections, several groups using faith to justify terrorism promise eternal salvation to those who participate. This is true not only of martyrs, as mentioned previously, but more broadly of those who participate in self-described battles for divine justice and to defend and promote the faith, including individuals that use terrorism.

Religions, however, are not only focused on eternal salvation. Faith traditions are also deeply concerned with what happens in this world, including practicing the faith correctly, what is known as orthopraxy, and confronting external threats to the faith, including other faith traditions. Under certain conditions, some groups come to believe that their faith is being corrupted from within, and they need to purify the religion of individuals who are not living up to a particular understanding of the faith. This is a phenomenon often called "fundamentalism," which will be described further in the next section. For example, a particular understanding of Sunni Islam known as *Salafism* aims to create one strict understanding and practice of the faith around the world (Wictorowicz 2006). At its most extreme, this movement helped inform the ideology of ISIL and its indiscriminate violence against fellow Muslims, namely Shia and secular Sunnis, which it sees as corrupting this one understand of the faith (McCants 2015). Religious groups can also target those outside their faith that they perceive to be a threat to their faith. For example, organizations of monks in Myanmar have aimed to rid the country of Muslim citizens that they believe do not have the right to live in the country and to fight what they believe to be a threat posed by Muslim expansion in general. These cases of earthly salvation will be further explored in Section 5.

Social Resources

In addition to scriptures and beliefs, religions tend to include key social resources that, under certain circumstances, can be useful tools for perpetuating acts of terrorism. Perhaps most importantly, religions have leaders.

Religious leaders are particularly powerful because they have moral authority that they receive from studying the faith tradition in depth, or through a special connection to the divine that gives them legitimacy. Sociologist Christian Smith (1996, 20) refers to this as "privileged legitimacy" and notes that "in many societies, organized religion enjoys a certain authority, legitimacy and protection not enjoyed by other social institutions and organizations. This is because religion deals with the sacred and supernatural and . . . it may have a history or current status as a socially powerful institution."

Religious leaders are especially important for understanding the conditions under which groups engage in violence and terrorism because, usually, they are the ones who interpret scriptures and stories in light of real-world events and provide direction on actions that the faithful should take to realize a better world. Furthermore, religious leaders are often skilled speakers, which make them powerful motivators, and religious leaders have experience organizing and managing groups of people (Gregg 2014b). Religious leaders, therefore, are a powerful resource for groups wishing to challenge the status quo, including through terrorism. The following sections will investigate the conditions under which religious leaders call for killing civilians as a necessary means of realizing various goals.

Furthermore, most religions create social networks that keep adherents in touch with one another and provide loose ties that bind them in faith. Gregg (2018, 197) notes that "religions . . . come with preexisting formal and informal networks of the faithful, through mosques, temples, churches, monastic orders, student unions, religious study groups, and so on." For example, the Roman Catholic Church boasts nearly 1.3 billion baptized members worldwide, 221,700 parishes, and almost 500,000 priests (Vatican Press Office 2018). As such, it is probably the single largest social network in the world. These networks can be powerful resources for spreading information, providing a sense of global community, and fostering identity and purpose (Gregg 2018). Religions also create social networks through charities, schools, humanitarian assistance programs, and other social services that provide resources to populations in addition to connecting them to one another. Furthermore, these networks are often transnational and extend beyond local communities and state borders, connecting people together spiritually and forming a shared sense of purpose and identity, what anthropologist Scott Atran (2010) calls "shared kinship." Finally, sociologist Christian Smith (1996) notes that religions come with readymade moral codes of conduct that help bind groups together and address deviance more quickly than groups that have to creates these norms from scratch. As will be described in the subsequent sections, various groups have used these resources to recruit, mobilize, and organize individuals for action, including acts of terrorism.

Religion and Material Resources

Finally, a broader definition of religion includes material resources that could be useful for organizing and mobilizing adherents and, under certain conditions, can help facilitate calls for acts of terrorism. For example, religions have buildings, including churches, mosques, temples, and so on, that could be used as hubs for meetings and to organize groups and actions. Religious groups also tend to have considerable financial resources, including charitable donations, such as tithing in Christianity, or zakat in Islam. Smith (1996, 16) calls these and other material resources "enterprise tools" that allow groups to mobilize, organize, and spread information. Under certain circumstances, these resources can be powerful tools for groups wishing to challenge the social and political landscape, including through terrorism (Gregg 2018).

Conclusion

In sum, a broader understanding of religion as complex faith systems that include ideological, social, and material resources, along with key beliefs, and a broader understanding of the purpose of religions that goes beyond peace, love, and ethical conduct, is important for understanding religiously motivated terrorism. However, this discussion still leaves unanswered why religiously motivated terrorism occurs at some points in time but not at others, and the conditions under which killing is not only justified but even encouraged.

The next section will propose four conditions under which leaders use religious resources to produce interpretations calling for terrorism in the name of faith and the resources that help enable groups to carry out these acts.

4 Causes of Religious Terrorism

The previous section proposed that religions are about much more than propagating peace, love, and ethical conduct. Rather, religions are complex systems of scriptures, stories, doctrines, and laws, along with social and material resources that, under certain conditions, can be useful tools for justifying, motivating, and perpetrating acts of terrorism. It is this readymade set of resources that makes religions particularly useful for justifying, motivating, and carrying out a variety of actions, including acts of terrorism.

This list of religious resources, however, leaves unanswered why groups choose terrorism as a means of challenging the world around them and how they come to believe that these acts are not only justified but necessary. To answer these questions, it is important to look beyond the faith system itself and include circumstances outside of religion and how these circumstances shape interpretations of the faith. In other words, acts of religious terrorism do not originate solely from scriptures, practices, and beliefs from within a faith. Rather, religious terrorism is a combination of factors and circumstances outside the faith – political, social, security, and economic factors – that shape the way individuals and groups see themselves, their faith, and the actions they need to take to realize their goals.

This section will consider four broad conditions under which religious resources become tools that justify and perpetuate terrorism: fundamentalist calls for purity, religious nationalists' aim to seize the state, radical attempts to hasten the apocalypse, and the conditions under which individuals become radicalized and take up these causes. Each of these causal arguments draws from key scholars across numerous academic disciplines to illustrate the conditions under which groups use religious resources to threaten or use violence indiscriminately against average people.

Fundamentalist Calls for Purity

Perhaps one of the most widely studied causes of religious violence and terrorism is a phenomenon that is usually called *fundamentalism*. Similar to terrorism, however, this term and its meaning are hotly debated. Some choose, rather, to call it *religious revivalism*, noting that *fundamentalism* is a negative term with Christian roots (Esposito 1995), while others call it *extremism* or *radicalism* (McCauley and Moshalenko 2008; Robins and Post 1997). Despite disagreements on what to call it and why, the causes of this type of religiously motivated violence are similar across definitions.

At its most basic, fundamentalists believe that there is an urgent need to get back to the basics – the "fundamentals of the faith" – which have been corrupted or lost by human interpretation and external influences. They advocate for a literal reading of scripture and assert that there is only one correct understanding of the faith, orthodoxy, and one right practice, orthopraxy (Almond et al, 2002). In other words, fundamentalists are as much about purifying the religion from within as they are about defending against outside ideas and practices that they find threatening to the faith.

Several scholars note that fundamentalism is a defensive reaction to specific, perceived threats. First, and most notably, fundamentalists react to the perceived threat posed by secularism and modernism. For example, Martin E. Marty and R. Scott Appleby (1995, 1), the editors of the five-part "Fudanemtalisms Project," argue that fundamentalism springs out of mainstream movements but that "'Fundamentalists' within these historic religious traditions, convinced of the conspiratorial nature of secularists and liberal religionists, adopt a set of strategies for fighting back against what it perceives as a concerted effort by secular states or elements within them to push people of religious consciousness and conscience to the margins of society." Similarly, Jonathan Fox (2004, 113) contends, "the two characteristics that define fundamentalism are its origins as a defensive reaction to modernity and the attempt to impose fundamentalist rules and standards of behavior on society as a whole in order to actualize this defense." Almond, Appleby, and Sivan (2002, 94) summarize, "In short, the threat to the religious tradition may come from the general process of modernization and secularization, from other religions and/or ethnic groups, from a secular state (imperial or indigenous) seeking to secularize and delimit the domain of the sacred, or from various combinations of these."

Fundamentalists, in other words, aim to defend their faith against perceived threats by getting back to what they believe to be the one true understanding of the faith. They aim to return the faith to a "golden age," a period when they believe the religion was practiced most perfectly and before it became corrupted by new interpretations or external threats

(Gregg 2016). Almond, Appleby, and Sivan (2002) note that, within this threat posed by external factors, fundamentalists are often highly critical of their own religious leadership, which they believe has become corrupted by these new influences. The authors argue, "In most cases these movements perceive their own compromising religious establishments as endangering the survival of the true religion" (2002, 100). Ultimately, therefore, fundamentalists aim to purify their faith from what they believe to be polluting elements, including threats internal to the faith (corrupt leadership, new interpretations, heterodoxy) and external threats, such as the rise of secularism and modernism, the introduction of new political systems that are believed to be marginalizing the religion, and the imposition of other faith systems. These perceived threats propel fundamentalists to take actions to protect what they believe to be the true understanding and practice of their religion.

Fundamentalists are not de facto violent. Fundamentalists may choose to isolate from wider society, either through physical isolation or socially by "creating parallel institutions, such as schools, clinics, stores, and so on" and "by creating distinct and highly visible forms of dress . . . that distinguish them from others within the faith and wider society," as the Amish in the United States and Ultra-Orthodox Jewish communities around the world have done (Gregg 2016, 346). Fundamentalists may also become politically active – including through elections, demonstrations, or attempting to change policies – as a means of challenging perceived threats to the faith. Evangelical Christians in the United States have chosen this path to address issues ranging from abortion to prayer in public schools.

Finally, fundamentalists may turn to terrorism if they are not able to retreat and isolate themselves from their perceived threats. They may also use terrorism if their path to purifying faith and wider society is blocked. At its most extreme, this bid for purity could lead to indiscriminate mass violence aimed at "cleansing the faith" from threats posed by diversity within the religion and wider society. For example, as will be described in Section 5, ISIL enacted a campaign of mass murder and terrorism that targeted not only those outside the faith, such as Yazidis and Christians, but also those within Islam, particularly Shia Muslims and secular Sunnis, which they deemed apostates and polluters of the purity of the faith.

Religious Nationalists' Aim to Seize the State

The 1979 Iranian Revolution, which took most scholars by surprise, successfully united large segments of the population with an ideology that used religious beliefs, practices, and resources, including the charismatic leadership of Ayatollah Khomeini. Juergensmeyer (1993) drew from this event to argue that, despite academic expectations to the contrary, religion was on a path to reasserting itself in politics around the globe. He identified several examples across religious traditions to make this assertion, including the 1984 standoff between Sikh militants and the Indian military that ended in a bloody confrontation at the Golden Temple in Amristar; Buddhist militancy in Sri Lanka that aimed, in part, to make Buddhism a key tenet of the government; the rise of Hindu nationalism in India and the creation of the Hindu-nationalist party, the BJP; and the birth of Hamas during the First Palestinian Intifada and its ultimate aim to make Islam the governing principle of a Palestinian state.

Juergensmeyer (1993) identifies several key causes for the reassertion of religion into political life. First, he argues that secular nationalism, or ideologies that aim to separate religion from politics and society, became a threat to religion's traditional role as a source of authority. Furthermore, secular nationalism made several promises for the developing world, including greater stability, economic prosperity, and the rights of citizens to choose their own leaders. Juergensmeyer argues that these promises were largely unfulfilled in the countries and regions in which secular nationalism was embraced, compelling intellectuals and average citizens to seek out alternative ideologies.

Under these conditions, movements in several countries created what he calls "religious nationalism" to compete with secular nationalism. "Both religious and secular-nationalistic frameworks of thought conceive of the world in coherent, manageable ways; they both suggest that there are levels of meaning beneath the day-to-day world that give coherence to things unseen; and they both provide the authority that gives the social and political order its reason for being" (Juergensmeyer 1993, 31). Juergensmeyer further notes that leaders claimed that religious nationalism was an authentic ideology, giving it a degree of legitimacy, whereas secular nationalism became viewed as foreign and forced by colonial and imperialist powers. He even goes so far as to assert that secularism became viewed as a Christian ideology, given its origins in the West, further delegitimizing its presence in non-Christian countries (Juergensmeyer 1993, 16–30). Under this complex mixture of political, ideological, and social circumstances, religious nationalism has emerged as a competing "ideology of order" to secular nationalism.

Religious nationalists are similar to fundamentalists in their aim to restore religion to public and political life but see a "top-down" approach as the necessary path to achieving their goals, including seizing the state. Religious nationalists further strive to make religion the grounding principle of the nation, placing religious affiliation over one's ethnic identity, class, or even citizenship. In other words, religious nationalists aim to create what anthropologist Benedict Anderson famously called "imagined communities" – large collectives of people that provide a sense of common identity, purpose, and community (Juergensmeyer 1993, 30).

Religious nationalists use terrorism to further these goals in several ways. First, violence against fellow citizens can be used to coerce others into joining the cause or at least complying with it. For example, the Islamic State created "morality police" that monitored average citizens for their compliance with Islamic laws, often using corporal punishment, including death, for those who violated the rules. Religious nationalists also have used terrorism to bait the state into over-reacting and punishing the general population, demonstrating its immorality and ill intentions towards its citizens. Both al-Qaeda and ISIL, for example, have been accused of using terrorism to provoke an overreaction from US, Canadian, and European governments, thus driving a deeper wedge between the West and Muslims (Cordesman 2016). Terrorism can also be used to show the weakness of the state. For example, despite the demise of the Islamic State in 2017 and the death of its leader, Abu Bakr al-Baghdadi, in 2019, ISIL continues to perpetrate terrorist acts in Iraq and Syria, demonstrating that security forces are unable to stop these attacks.

Hastening the Apocalypse

As described in Section 3, most religious traditions have expectations that this world will end, what Christianity calls the apocalypse, and that a period of peace and harmony will replace it, or the millennium. This expectation of the end of times, despite its promise of suffering and bloodshed, holds tremendous hope for the faithful that divine judgment and justice will prevail and all wrongs will be made right. It is this hope that produces what terrorism expert Ehud Sprinzak (1992, 48) calls "catastrophic messianism," or the belief not only that the end of times is near but that individuals and groups may hasten the end and turn the battle in their favor, bringing about divine justice and peace. This phenomenon is also known as "cosmic war" (Juergensmeyer 2000) and "apocalyptic war" (Gregg 2018).

Scholars suggest several conditions under which individuals and groups might turn toward hastening the apocalypse. Robert S. Robins and Jerrold M. Post (1997, 113) posit that "the individual whose world is falling apart is experiencing his own psychological apocalypse. From this state of powerlessness and meaninglessness, some create a world of meaning in their mind, a new world in which they have meaning and significance. Through this vision they have found personal redemption." More specifically, Robins and Post argue that two events produce apocalyptic thinking: "the oppressive occupation of one people by another, with the apocalyptic vision bringing hope to the oppressed; and periods of social decay, with the apocalyptic vision as an antidote to immoral and irreligious behavior" (1997, 113). Juergensmeyer (2000, 162) identifies three causes of apocalyptic thinking: a group's very identity is believed to be under imminent attack, losing the battle would be "unthinkable," and "the struggle is blocked and cannot be won in real time or in real terms." Under these conditions, earthly battles become spiritual battles in which the faithful must participate. Juergensmeyer further argues, "To live in a state of [cosmic] war is to live in a world in which individuals know who they are, why they have suffered, by whose hand they have been humiliated, and at what expense they have persevered" (2000, 155).

Charismatic leaders play a critical role in transforming expectations of the apocalypse into active participants in apocalyptic war. Specifically, charismatic leaders identify real-world events, connect them to expectations of the end of times, and instruct followers in the actions they should take for their own salvation, including violence and terrorism. Rapoport (1999), for example, contends that, in order for apocalyptic war to take hold, signs of the end of time and the need for urgent action must be exaggerated and this exaggeration is the result of leaders. Robins and Post (1997, 114–115) argue, "For the followers, such an inspired leader has provided a diagnosis of the ills afflicting the world and has given them a special role to play. He has made sense for them of the surrounding chaos." Gregg (2016, 349) asserts, "leaders use scriptures and the expectation of the end times to offer an explanation for the suffering and trials of current situations and what individuals should do in order to liberate themselves, spiritually and literally, from these trying circumstances."

Individuals and groups attempting to foment the apocalypse, almost by definition, anticipate violence; they expect and even long for the epic battles and bloodshed that they believe will bring the end of time and usher in divine justice and peace. Terrorist acts, particularly those that perpetrate mass chaos and bloodshed, create these conditions. As will be described in Section 5, Aum Shinrikyo's 1995 attack on a Tokyo subway aimed to unleash World War III, the destruction of the world, and salvation for its followers. Similarly, white supremacists dream of a "racial holy war" (RAHOWA), designed to cleanse the world of what they believe are polluting elements of the human race.

Finally, it is important to point out that not all groups anxiously awaiting the apocalypse are violent. Jewish mystics, Kabbalists, "have been instructed through the ages to keep hope in their millennialist expectations, but that the end will not be revealed beforehand, nor will it be the result of human will; their job is to be faithful and vigilant" (Gregg 2016, 349). The Millerite Movement in nineteenth-century United States predicted the second coming of Jesus between 1843 and 1845 but was neither violent leading up to Jesus's expected return nor after, when these expectations were unmet (Knight 1993). Apocalyptic warriors are different in that they believe their actions, including mass violence, will help hasten the end of times and usher in the millennium.

The Path to Radicalization

Within these broader causes of religious terrorism, several academic fields, including psychology, social psychology, and anthropology, have explored the conditions under which individuals become radicalized and how radicalization leads to violent behavior, especially terrorism. These explanations usually focus on the individual and aim to understand the complex mixture of psychological and environmental factors that propel individuals to join extremist groups that perpetrate acts of violence with some of the goals outline previously.

Several scholars argue that causes of radicalization need to distinguish between radicalization of beliefs and radicalization of actions. For example, Randy Borum (2011, 30) argues, "*Radicalization* – the process of developing extremist ideologies and beliefs – needs to be distinguished from *action pathways* – the process of engaging in terrorism or violent extremist actions." Similarly, Peter Neumann (2013) distinguishes between what he calls "cognitive radicalization," which is the process of adopting radical beliefs, and "behavior radicalization," which are violent actions. Psychologist John Horgan (2009, 152) differentiates between what he calls radicalization and violent radicalization. He defines radicalization as "the social and psychological process of incrementally experienced commitment to extremist political or religious ideology. Radicalization may not necessarily lead to violence, but is one of several risk factors required for this." Horgan then defines violent radicalization as "*increased* and *focused* radicalization" and that it "encompasses the stages of a) becoming involved with a terrorist group and, b) remaining involved and becoming involved in terrorist activities" (2009, 152). Horgan's definitions therefore rely on progressive stages that increasingly radicalize individuals to the point of violence.

Psychologists Clark McCauley's and Sophia Moskalenko's (2017, 211) political radicalization "two pyramid model" also stresses the importance of distinguishing "radicalization of opinion from radicalization of action." Their "opinion pyramid" is based on "neutral" people, followed by "sympathizers" who believe in the cause but not violence, then "justifiers" that support violent action, and finally those who feel a "*personal moral obligation*" to take up violence in defense of the cause" (2017, 212, emphasis theirs). The "action pyramid" has "inert" supporters (the base of the pyramid), "activists" in the middle, "radicals" higher up, and "terrorists" at the top. McCauley and Moshalenko (2008, 418) also articulate three levels of radicalization – individual, group and mass – with a total of twelve "drivers" of extremism, ranging from personal victimization and political grievances at the personal level, to intergroup and intragroup rivalries at the group level, to "jujutsu politics" (in-group radicalization through the construction of outgroup threats), including hate and martyrdom at the mass level. Their work, in other words, distinguishes between beliefs and actions, as well as drivers of individual and group radicalization.

Psychologist Fathali Mohammad Moghaddam (2005) also describes a process for incremental radicalization that culminates with violence – what he calls a "staircase to the terrorist act" – as an explanation of radicalization. His model is divided into six "floors," beginning with the ground floor, which includes the general population who, by and large, find their circumstances to be fair and thus stay on the ground floor. The first floor contains individuals who believe they can improve their circumstances and is divided between those who believe that they can do this nonviolently versus those who believe violence is necessary. The second floor is occupied by those with violent tendencies who are searching for someone or something on which blame their dissatisfaction. The third floor holds those who are considering violent acts as part of a wider campaign believed to promote justice and fairness. The fourth floor further isolates the individual from his or her family and friends and dehumanizes the "other." And the fifth floor contains individuals who perpetrate act of terrorism. Ultimately, his model is designed to explain the process in which individuals with grievances are willing to use violence against fellow citizens.

Political scientists Mohammed Hafez and Creighton Mullins (2015, 958) challenge Moghaddam's progression model, arguing rather that that terrorist need four pieces of a "puzzle" to turn to violent action: "personal and collective grievances, networks and interpersonal ties, political and religious ideologies, and enabling environments and support structures." Focusing specifically on radicalization in the West, the authors also note the importance of distinguishing beliefs from actions and the critical role that religion plays in informing ideologies. "In the case of religious extremists, ideology can frame personal sacrifice in this world as a steppingstone to eternal salvation and redemption. The rewards of afterlife far exceed any possible pleasures that can be derived in this world" (2015, 967).

Robbins and Post (1997) think of radicalism in terms of a dynamic between psychologically wounded leaders and needy followers that form a "lock and key" relationship that can lead to radicalism. The authors propose that during times of prolonged stress, uncertainty, and fear, populations may look to a charismatic leader to provide assurance and guidance, including especially religious leaders who can situate the chaos in a spiritual context. "Some people on the verge of psychological collapse," they argue, "find comfort and meaning in a highly structured religious belief system" (1997, 114). Furthermore, enlisting followers helps the wounded leader. They argue, "His delusion is sense-making not only for him but also for other wounded individuals whose world is falling apart ... for the followers, such an inspired leader has provided a diagnosis of the ills afflicting the world and has given them a special role to play" (1997, 114). Under these conditions, and especially if the leader is both paranoid and has a "messianic delusion," he or she can be the inspiration for violence, including terrorism, to further his or her goals.

Wiktorowicz (2005) also focuses on the importance of leadership in the process of radicalization. He identifies three stages of radicalization. The first process is "cognitive opening and religious seeking," in which individuals respond to some sort of crisis (including losing a job, experiencing discrimination, or perceiving political disenfranchisement). Wictorowicz notes that once a cognitive opening occurs, the individual may undergo a "religious seeking process ... in which an individual searches for some satisfactory system of religious meaning to interpret and resolve discontent" (2005, 21). The second stage is "reputation and sacred authority," in which individuals become willing to listen to leaders' interpretations of scripture and law. He notes that, in Islam, authority is usually determined by religious training and reputation (2005, 24–26). And the third stage is "culturing and commitment," in which extremists socialize individuals to the group's message and behavior. Wictorowicz stresses that the ultimate goal of these groups is to "prompt religious ideological conversion" (2005, 21).

Finally, anthropologist Scott Atran (2010) provides a different argument for radicalization. He posits that the need for community and "brotherhood" is a key driver of those joining extremist groups, including individuals that perpetrate terrorist acts against innocent people. Atran writes, "It is the larger family, or 'tribe,' and not the mostly ordinary individuals in it, that increasingly has seemed to me the key to understanding the extraordinary violence of mass killing and the murder of innocents." Atran further explains that his use of "tribe" does not refer to the anthropological sense of connection through blood but "a group of interlinked communities that largely share a common cultural sense of themselves, and which imagine and believe themselves to be part of one big family and home" (2010, 8–9). Atran further proposes, "Maybe people don't kill and die simply for a cause. They do it for friends – campmates, schoolmates, workmates," what Atran calls "imagined kin" (2010, 11). Radicalization, in other words, is not about ideological conversion or even eternal salvation but about finding camaraderie, identity, and "family."

Conclusion

The four broad conditions outlined herein – fundamentalist calls for purity, religious nationalists' aim to seize the state, radical attempts to hasten the apocalypse, and the conditions under which individuals become radicalized and take up these causes – help explain how religious resources become tools that justify and perpetuate terrorism. The next section will use these broad causes of religious terrorism to analyze five cases across several faith traditions to better illustrate the conditions under which these acts of violence occur.

5 Examples of Religious Terrorism across Faith Traditions

Section 4 provided a discussion on the conditions under which individuals and groups resort to terrorism in the name of faith. It outlined four broad arguments of religiously motivated terrorism in particular: fundamentalist calls for purity, religious nationalists' aim to seize the state, radical attempts to foment the apocalypse, and the conditions under which individuals take up these calls and become radicalized.

This section offers brief descriptions of five groups that have drawn on religious resources to justify and perpetuate acts of terrorism. First, it considers the rise of ISIL, its use of a particular understanding of Islam called *Salafism*, and the conditions under which it has justified brutal acts of violence against civilians and the slaughter of thousands. Second, it provides a brief overview of Identity Christianity and how it helped spawn the white supremacy movement in the United States, which has targeted various minority groups with terrorist acts. Third, this section looks at the conditions under which Buddhist monks formed the 969 Movement and Ma-Ba-Tha in Myanmar; their use of Buddhism to justify calls for ridding the country of Muslims, fueling a military crackdown on Muslims, particularly in the state of Rakhine; and citizen-led attacks against Muslims throughout the country. Fourth, it outlines the conditions that led to the creation of the Jewish Defense League in the United States, how this group justified violence against civilians in the United States and Israel, and its lasting legacy. Finally, the section looks at an example of a "New Religious Movement" – Aum Shinrikyo – and its use of a hybrid of religious beliefs to justify attacking Japanese civilians with a chemical weapon in 1995.

These cases aim to illustrate the conditions under which groups use religious resources to justify and motivate religious violence and terrorism more specifically. To do this, it draws on cases from several religious traditions, including Islam, Christianity, Buddhism, Judaism, and a "new" religion (Aum Shinrikyo). Furthermore, these cases represent some of the most prominent examples of terrorism done in the name of faith. ISIL remains a global security threat, despite the loss of its caliphate and leader, Abu Bakr al-Baghdadi, and its use of terrorism continues to affect populations around the globe. Aum Shinrikyo's 1995 attack on the Tokyo subway system represents one of the few cases of a nonstate actor deploying WMD in a terrorist act. Buddhist monks' calls for indiscriminate acts of violence against Muslim citizens in Myanmar has helped produce one of the largest forced migrations in the twenty-first century. Meir Kahane, the founder of the Jewish Defense League, developed an ideology calling for violence as a necessary tool of religious purification that has continued long beyond his lifetime. And white supremacists have built on a fringe interpretation of Christianity to foment a call for racial war as a necessary means of cleansing the human race of "impure" elements. These cases, in other words, provide a glimpse into the conditions under which religion is weaponized, why terrorism is employed, and how these ideas persist over time.

ISIL

In 2013, a group calling itself *ad-Dawlah al-Islāmiyah fī 'l-ʿIrāq wa-sh-Shām*, which translates into the Islamic State of Iraq and the Levant or ISIL, began to assert its independence from al-Qaeda affiliates in Syria, roughly two years after the beginning of its civil war. Within a year, ISIL had managed to capture territory in Syria and, in 2014, began to take cities in Iraq, culminating with the capture of Mosul in June of 2014. On June 29, ISIL's leader, Abu Bakr al-Baghdadi, proclaimed the return of the Islamic caliphate, or an Islamic state governed by himself as the caliph, or its rightly guided leader. ISIL not only imposed a harsh understanding of Islamic law (Sharia) but also began to slaughter Shias, Yazidis, Christians, and secular Sunnis by the thousands (Kilcullen 2016, 139–140). Around the world, insurgent groups espousing a similar ideology to ISIL pledged their allegiance to the self-appointed caliph and began to carry out similar acts against civilians, including Boko Haram in Nigeria, Abu Sayyef Group in the Philippines, IS-Khorasan in Pakistan and Afghanistan, and several groups in Libya, to name a few. Simultaneously, tens of thousands of foreign fighters, including more than five thousand from Europe alone, began to pour into Syria and Iraq, with the ambition of joining the caliphate and fighting on behalf of the Islamic State (Barrett 2017).

The Islamic State was all but defeated by the end of 2018, having lost its territory in Iraq and Syria, and in 2019, US forces killed its leader, Abu Bakr al-Baghdadi. Despite these significant setbacks, affiliate groups and the overarching ideology have remained, with individual sympathizers vowing to carry out terrorist acts against civilians in Europe, the United States, Canada, and beyond. What conditions led to the emergence of ISIL? What are its goals? And how has religion informed its actions?

ISIL emerged in the wake of failed efforts to stabilize Iraq after the US-led invasion in 2003. Multiple insurgent groups formed in Iraq to fight the invasion and the emergence of the new Shia-dominated government, including especially al-Qaeda in Iraq, which was run by Jordanian-born Abu Musab al-Zarqawi. Al-Qaeda in Iraq carried out several large terrorist attacks, including the 2005 bombing of several hotels in Amman, Joran, which killed sixty people, and the 2006 bombing of the Shia Al-Askari Mosque in Samarra, which set off tit-for-tat attacks between Sunni and Shia communities that left thousands dead (Kilcullen 2016, 29). Al-Qaeda in Iraq briefly declared a state in 2006, with Anbar as its capital; however, it was short-lived. Following the assassination of Zarqawi that same year, the withdrawal of US troops from Iraq in 2011, and the outbreak of the civil war in Syria, al-Qaeda in Iraq joined forces with the Nusra front in Syria, which was allied with al-Qaeda, before eventually breaking away from al-Qaeda and creating ISIL in 2013 (McCants 2015).

ISIL has both earthly and eternal goals for which it claims to be fighting. First, ISIL aims to unify the worldwide Muslim community, the umma, under one understanding of the faith. Initially, the Muslim community was united under the Prophet Muhammed, followed by the first four caliphs (Abu Bakr, Omar, Othman, and Ali). However, after Ali was murdered in 661 CE, and a bloody battle between Muslim factions in Karbala occurred in 680 CE, the community formally split between those who recognized the caliph as the legitimate form of leadership, the Sunnis, and those who believed leadership should be determined by the bloodline to the Prophet Muhammed, the Shias. ISIL's declaration of the caliphate in 2014 aimed to reunify the community under one polity (McCants 2015).

ISIL's earthly goals also aim to "purify" Islam. As Islam spread around the world, it adopted local practices and customs, making the faith diverse. For example, Sufis, Islam's mystics, spread the faith throughout South Asia and encouraged the inclusion of local practices, including music and dance, as part of worship and devotion to God – practices that more orthodox understandings of Islam forbid. ISIL strives to rid Islam of these "heterodox" practices by embracing and promoting a particular understanding of the faith known as *Salafism*. Salafism purports that the Qur'an and Sunna (the sayings, or Hadith, and actions of the Prophet Muhammed) are sufficient for instructing the Muslim community today and that human reason is *bidah*, or innovation. Quintan Wictorowicz (2006, 207) explains, "Salafis believe that by strictly following the rules and guidance in the Qur'an and Sunna (path or example of the Prophet Muhammad) they eliminate the biases of human subjectivity and self-interest, thereby allowing them to identify the singular truth of God's commands ... from this perspective, there is only one legitimate religious interpretation; Islamic pluralism does not exist."

ISIL further aims to purify and unify Islam through a doctrine in Islam known as the "Prophetic Methodology." Graeme Wood (2015, 4) describes, "Virtually every major decision and law promulgated by the Islamic State adheres to what it calls, in its press and pronouncements, and on its billboards, license plates, stationery, and coins, "the Prophetic methodology," which means following the prophecy and example of Muhammad, in punctilious detail." This includes a wide array of activities, ranging from wearing a beard, as the Prophet Muhammed did, to keeping slaves, which was practiced during his lifetime. ISIL, in other words, is using a particular interpretation of the Prophet's actions to explain and justify its behavior to the wider Muslim community.

Furthermore, ISIL's aim to purify and unify the umma actually may be a means to apocalyptic ends. ISIL draws heavily from signs of the apocalypse to speak to the Muslim world and gain support. William McCants (2015) notes that ISIL's use of a black flag conforms to an apocalyptic expectation from an early Islamic scholar who predicted, "The black banners will come from the East, led by men like mighty camels, with long hair and long beards; their surnames are taken from the names of their hometowns" (26). Furthermore, Wood (2015) observes that ISIL has drawn on an apocalyptic prediction of a major battle with "Rome" in the city of Dabiq (in present day Syria) to call for a military confrontation with US and coalition forces, as well as the prediction of another battle in "Constantinople," followed by the falling away of the faithful to a mere 5,000, and then a final battle in Jerusalem in which Jesus will intervene on behalf of faithful Muslims to explain their actions and motivate followers (Wood 2015, McCants 2015).

ISIL's former leader, Abu Bakr al-Baghdadi, is another important figure that drew on apocalyptic expectations and religious credentials for his legitimacy. Al-Baghdadi traced his lineage to the Quraysh tribe, the Prophet Muhammed's tribe, which McCants (2015, 74, 116) notes is important for fulfilling an apocalyptic expectation that twelve rightly guided caliphs will govern the umma before the end of times. Esposito (2003, 49) notes that only with a rightly guided caliph are some aspects of Sharia implementable. Al-Baghdadi's recreation of the caliphate, with himself as its leader, therefore, was also a means of implementing what ISIL claims to be the most perfect form of Sharia on earth (Wood 2015). Finally, al-Baghdadi held a PhD in Qur'anic recitation from the University of Baghdad, which further gave him a degree of religious legitimacy.

Importantly, several sources suggest that many Muslims may currently have apocalyptic expectations. For example, McCants (2015, 27) notes that "apocalyptic messages resonate among many Muslims today because of the political turmoil in the Middle East." Specifically, McCants cites a 2012 survey by the Pew Foundation, which found that more than half of the adult Muslims asked in nine of twenty-three countries surveyed believe that the return of the Mahdi (a figure that marks the beginning of the period of judgment, sometimes believed to be Jesus) was about to happen, which are signs that the Muslim apocalypse is near. In Afghanistan, the number that believed the end of times was near was 82 percent; in Iraq, 72 percent; in Turkey, 68 percent; and in Tunisia, 67 percent (Bell 2012, 58). Therefore, several Muslim populations may be actively looking for signs of the end of times, presenting an opportunity for ISIL's apocalyptic message to be heard.

To build its base and increase its religious legitimacy, ISIL called on Muslims from all over the globe to perform the *hijra* – to immigrate to the caliphate – and fight on behalf of the Islamic State. As early as 2011, foreign fighters began migrating to Syria from neighboring countries including Libya, Jordan, and Turkey. The Soufan Center, which tracks foreign fighters connected to ISIL, estimated that more than 40,000 foreign fighters came to the Islamic State from more than 110 countries in all, and nearly 20,000 women and children came to support the effort (Barrett 2017).

Furthermore, the Soufan Center estimates that more than 5,000 fighters traveled from Europe, with France supplying 1,900 fighters alone (Barrett 2017, 10).

To achieve its goals, ISIL perpetrated a range of terrorist acts designed to cleanse the faith and the *dar al Islam*, the territory of Islam, from religious impurities. In Iraq and Syria, ISIL targeted Shia Muslims, which it deems de facto as apostates (McCants 2015). ISIL also targeted Sufis, Islamic mystics, and some of the first sites ISIL destroyed after invading Iraq were Sufi shrines (Isakhan and Zarandona 2017). Furthermore, ISIL killed fellow Sunnis, especially more secular minded Sunnis, whom it also deemed apostates (Williams 2016, 285–288; Haykel 2015, 21–26). Outside the faith, ISIL targeted Christians, Yazidis, and any other religious group that stood in its way. Overall, the UN estimates that ISIL murdered at least 15,000 in Iraq and Syria and, as of 2018, 202 mass graves have been found in Iraq alone (United Nations 2018).

Similar patterns are visible with ISIL affiliates around the globe. ISIL in the Sinai Peninsula murdered 305 Sufi worshipers while in prayer at a mosque in 2017, in addition to numerous attacks that killed Coptic Christians in Egypt (Walsh and Yussef 2017). In the Philippines, ISIL elements seized and held the city of Marawi in Mindanao for five months between May and June of 2017. The Armed Forces of the Philippines had to virtually destroy the city to rout out ISIL forces and, despite killing its leader, second in command and numerous other fighters, ISIL regrouped and appointed a new leader within months (Straits Times 2018). In West Africa, Boko Haram – the insurgent group that kidnapped 276 schoolgirls from Chibook in 2014 – pledged allegiance to ISIL in 2015, causing the organization to split. ISIL in West Africa Province has continued to target civilians in Borno State in Nigeria, in addition to attacks in Chad, Cameroon, and Niger. As of 2018, the Nigeria Security Tracker claims that Boko Haram has been responsible for more than 37,500 deaths as part of the broader conflict it has caused (Campbell and Harwood 2018). A similar pattern is visible with ISIL in Khorasan, which straddles Pakistan and Afghanistan. Since its formation in 2015, it has killed thousands in terrorist attacks in both countries (Center for Strategic and International Studies 2018).

Finally, ISIL has made terrorist attacks in the West one of its priorities. In 2014, Abu Mohammed al Adnani, the spokesperson for ISIL, issued a statement that instructed, "If you can kill a disbelieving American or Canadian . . . smash his head with a rock, or slaughter him with a knife, or run him over with your car, or throw him down from a high place, or choke him, or poison him" (Bayoumy 2014). Numerous individuals have perpetrated terrorist acts in the West without any formal connection to ISIL, and the Soufan Center notes that twice as many attacks in the West have been perpetrated by individuals with no formal connection to ISIL than those with direct ties (Barrett 2017). A short list of such attackers includes Syed Rizwan and Tashfin Farooq, who killed fourteen in San Bernadino in 2015; Omar Mateen, the perpetrator of the 2016 Pulse Nightclub shooting that killed forty-nine; and Mohamed Salmene Lahouaiej-Bouhlel, who was responsible for the 2016 Bastille Day killing of eighty-six in Nice, France, to name but a few examples (Williams 2016, 276–281). These individuals received inspiration but no formal training from ISIL.

The conditions under which ISIL emerged, its use of Islam and its goals can be explained by several of the arguments for causes of religious terrorism outlined in Section 4. First, ISIL has drawn on a literal understanding of Islam, Salafism, to unify and purify the worldwide Muslim community through what they purport to be the one true understanding of the faith, conforming to fundamentalists' call for purifying the faith. ISIL has taken this goal to the greatest extremes, murdering not only those outside the faith that reside within the *dar al Islam* but also those within Islam, including Shia, Sufis, and secular Muslims – all of whom they deem apostates. ISIL's further aimed to seize the state in order to impose their religious principles on the country. ISIL aimed to hold territory, establish the Islamic State, recreate the caliphate, and then purify the Muslim world with the help of like-minded groups that pledged their allegiance to the caliph. Finally, ISIL has drawn heavily from apocalyptic expectations outlined in the traditions of Islam to signal to the umma the impending end of times and the need for Muslims' participation to achieve eternal salvation. As a 2012 Pew survey suggests, considerable numbers surveyed believe that the end of days is near. These apocalyptic expectations may provide a "cognitive opening," described by scholars of radicalization, that helps ISIL's promises of divine justice and salvation take hold.

Identity Christians and White Supremacism

In the United States, white supremacy – sometimes called white nationalism, the far right, or alt-right – is an ideology that draws, in part, on a particular interpretation of Christianity, known as Identity Christianity. As noted previously, this ideology claims that white Anglo-Saxons are the true chosen people of God, and, Jews and people of color are the offspring of Satan. While Identity Christianity and white supremacy are fringe movements that have little-to-no credibility with the larger Christian community, they appear to be on the rise in the United States, Canada, and Europe. For example, the 2017 "Unite the Right" protest in Charlottesville, Virginia, brought thousands of white supremacists out into the open, chanting phrases like "Jews will not replace us" and producing violent clashes with counter-protestors that left one dead. That same year, the Anti-Defamation League reported a record number of anti-Semitic incidents in the United States, up 57 percent from the year before (Anti-Defamation League 2017). And in 2019, the director of the FBI said white supremacy was "a persistent, pervasive threat" to the United States (Cohen 2019). How does Christianity inform this racist ideology and its acts of terrorism? What are white supremacists' goals?

Several scholars assert that Christianity in the West has a long and troubled history of racial superiority within its belief system, and that specific interpretations have helped justify colonialism, slavery, eugenics, Nazism, and white supremacy (Davis 2010, Fletcher, 2017, Serwer 2019). Identity Christianity and white supremacy, in fact, are not new belief systems. Their origins stretch back to seventeenth-century Britain and John Sadler's *Rights of the Kingdom*, in which he argued that the English were members of one of the ten lost tribes of Israel and therefore actually the true Israelites, whereas the Jews were Canaanites and not part of Israel. This idea was picked up by Richard Brothers at the end of the eighteenth century and then by John Wilson in the nineteenth century, who further developed the argument to include which lost tribes populated specific parts of Europe and that the Old Testament (the Hebrew Bible) was actually an account of White Anglo-Saxons and not the Jews. This ideology became known as British-Israelism (Barkun 1997; Davis 2010; Sharpe 2000).

Several factors gave rise to this extreme interpretation of Christian scriptures. In Britain, Davis (2010, 12) points to British expansionism and colonialization as a factor that led some scholars to devise claims of British racial and intellectual superiority relative to their colonial subjects. British Israelism also glommed onto conspiracy theories that Jews aimed to undermine Europe through the banking system, capitalizing on a long-standing anti-Semitic belief about Jewish people and finance (Davis 2010).

In the United States, the Identity Christian movement, which sprang from British-Israelism, became an influential articulation of this fusion of Christianity with race. Tanya Telfair Sharpe (2000) argues that Identity Christians adhere to British-Israelism's principle that Anglo-Saxons are the true Israelites and the idea that Jews and people of color are literal descendants of Satan – what is known as a polygenist or "two-seed" understanding of humanity. Michael Barkun (1997, xi) asserts, "Identity believes that Jews are not only wholly unconnected to the Israelites, but are the very children of the Devil, the literal biological offspring of a sexual dalliance between Satan and Eve in the Garden of Eden." Therefore, it is the responsibility of the true Israelites not to mix their seed with the children of Satan (Aho 1990, 85–86).

Identity Christianity further draws on a particular interpretation of the Bible and apocalyptic themes to inform its belief system. Sharpe (2000), for example, notes that Identity Christians adhere to a literal understanding of the King James Version of the Bible and the belief that the world is in the end of times. Barkun (1997, 104) also emphasizes their millennial nature, specifying that Identity Christianity "far from wishing to avoid this period of tumult, yearns for an opportunity to engage the forces of evil in an apocalyptic battle." Finally, Sharpe (2000, 606) stresses that the Identity Christian movement possesses "an antigovernment, paramilitary survivalist/conspiracy mentality based on a fear of the elimination of the White race" or what is also known as "white genocide." Within this apocalyptic anxiety is the belief that the US government, infiltrated by Jews, has created the "Zionist Occupational Government" (Barkun 1997, 111).

Several individuals developed and spread Identity Christian ideology in the United States. Joseph Wilde was perhaps the first American to shape these ideas, authoring several books in the late 1800s, as did Charles A. L. Totten, a West Point graduate and former lecturer at Yale University. In 1916 Madison Grant published *The Passing of the Great Race*, which argued that the Nordic race was responsible for humanity's great achievements, including the birth of the United States, and that it was under threat from immigration and the mixing of the races. These arguments helped spur congress to pass laws restricting immigration in the 1920s (Serwer 2019, 3–4). Works like these inspired the writings of J. H. Allen, who formed the Church of God (Holiness) to propagate early forms of white supremacy. Howard Rand created the Anglo-Saxon Federation of America in the 1930s and opened offices across the country to spread Identity beliefs (Davis 2010, 16–18). And William J. Cameron, publicist for Henry Ford and his motor company, used his skills as a journalist as well as his business and financial contacts to propagate Identity ideology around the country (Barkun 1997, 33–40). In Vancouver, British Columbia, a like-minded strain of Identity Christians, including H. Ben Judah and C. F. Parker, were active in the 1930s and 1940s, spreading the ideology to Washington state and Oregon (Barkun 1997, 51–52).

Following World War II, William Porter Gale, a retired army colonel who was on General McArthur's staff, attended the Anglo-Saxon Christian Congregation near Los Angeles (later renamed the Church of Jesus Christ, Christian) led by William Swift, a major proponent of Identity Christianity (Davis 2010, 21). Together with Conrad Gaard and Betrand Comparet, these four individuals became the key architects of the modern Christian Identity movement in the United State (Barkun 1997). They pointed to events in history as examples of a great conspiracy designed to threaten the "true" Israelites, including the creation of the Federal Reserve in 1913, which they believe were Jewish attempts to take over the government through finance (Aho 1990, 91). They further named the removal of money from the gold standard, the digitization of finance, and the creation of credit cards as a means of tracking and controlling individuals. Aho (1990, 91) notes that Identity Christians claim that these events are the fulfillment of a passage in Revelations, "and no man might buy or sell, save he that has the mark, or the name of the beast [i.e., of the bank]." Many white supremacists also believe that international organizations, like the United Nations, are plotting to create a "New World Order" designed to rob individuals of their liberties and identities. Finally, the election of Barak Obama to the highest office in the land, an African American, is believed to have created a more recent battle cry for white supremacists to rise up and fight the government (Jones 2018).

As an ideology, Identity Christianity has several goals. Perhaps chief among them is to spark a race war with the ultimate goal of ushering in a new era, the millennium. Sharpe (2000, 608) argues, "Identity followers believe that wars between and among the races will lead to an Aryan victory and restructuring of society that will reinstate the White man to his dominant place on earth and thereby restore 'order,'" and they often don the "battle cry 'RAHOWA' (Racial Holy War)" in their speeches and publications. Tied to this expectation, Identity Christian adherents prepare for this race war by embracing survivalist techniques, including stockpiling weapons, creating caches of food and other necessities, and even practicing paramilitary tactics and drills (Sharpe 2000, 608).

Identity Christians have created numerous groups aimed at realizing a race war and purifying the United States. Following World War I, early strains of Identity beliefs helped resuscitate the Ku Klux Klan, originally formed in Tennessee in 1865, and gave it a revival that spread from the South across the United States (Barkun 1997, 22–26). After World War II, several loosely organized groups formed, most of which were subject to infighting and only lasted a short time. Posse Comitatus, founded in the 1960s as a loose federation of militias, aimed to prepare white supremacists for armed conflict and teach survivalist techniques. In 1971, James Dennis Ellison founded the Covenant, Sword and Arm of the Lord in Missouri (which later moved to Arkansas), with the aim of training individuals in paramilitary techniques and spreading Identity beliefs. The FBI laid siege to their compound in 1985 under firearms violations and negotiated the peaceful surrender of its members, which effectively ended the organization (Nobel 2011). Aryan Nations, founded by Richard Butler in 1977, built off of Identity Christian ideology to create a paramilitary organization with chapters across the country. Butler also founded the Church of Jesus Christ

Christians alongside Aryan Nations (Aho 1990, 55–61). Robert J. Mathews, a disciple of Butler, founded the Order in 1983, which quickly dissolved after its members were prosecuted for several criminal acts (Aho 1990, 61–67).

Alongside these various groups were collections of like-minded individuals that functioned more like a movement and less like organizations. The Phineas Priesthood, or Phineas Priests, were a nonstructured collection of actors who carried out attacks, mostly in the Pacific Northwest, against individuals that they believed to be threatening the "white race." Danny Davis (2010, 45) argues that these individuals functioned more like "leaderless resistance, associate resistance or [a] Lone Wolf" inspired by Identity ideology than an organization. Other nonstructured collections of likeminded groups include neo-Nazis and Skinheads, who formed various short-lived groups, such as the National Alliance and the Hammerskin Nation (Perliger 2012).

Militant Identity Christians have used terrorist acts to target several groups that they see as a threat to the "white nation." Jewish citizens are a principal target and various white supremacists have repeatedly targeted synagogues and other Jewish sites. African Americans and people of color are another key target, ranging from acts of the KKK to the 2015 murder of nine African Americans at the Emmanuel African Methodist Episcopal Church in Charleston, South Carolina, perpetrated by a twenty-one-year-old self-proclaimed white supremacist (Blinder and Sack 2017). Interracial couples and homosexuals are another target. Skinheads, in particular, targeted homosexuals throughout the 1980s (Perliger 2012). White supremacists have also targeted, broadly, the US government and law enforcement agencies. The 1994 bombing of the Alfred P. Murrah Federal Building in Oklahoma City was the result of four individuals "motivated by their rage, frustration and resentment towards the federal government" (Perliger 2012, 10). Perlinger's (2012, 87) statistical analysis of violent attacks perpetrated by what he calls "the Far Right" in America identifies an exponential increase of attacks in the first eleven years of the new millennium, when compared to the 1990s.

Perhaps more important that the specific groups that have formed under the banner of white supremacy is the enduring ideas of racial purity, hatred of Jews and people of color, and acute paranoia of the government, ideas that stem, in part, by a particular reading of Christian scriptures. Former Grand Wizard of the KKK and member of the American Nazi Party Don Black created the website *Stormfront* in the 1990s, with the aim of linking together white supremacists and spreading their propaganda (Saslow 2018). Together with former Louisiana State Assembly Member David Duke, they have helped bring white supremacy more into the mainstream by calling themselves "white nationalists," downplaying violence, and developing a plan to create pure, white, Christian states (Saslow 2018). In 2008, Richard Bertram Spencer coined the term "alt-right" to describe a movement "whose core belief is that 'white identity' is under attack by multicultural forces using 'political correctness' and 'social justice' to undermine white people and 'their' civilization" (Southern Poverty Law Center 2019a). The alt-right has focused heavily on building an online presence and working through various media outlets to spread their ideology.

The persistence of white supremacy and its use of Christian scriptures to shape its ideology and justify terrorism are explained by several of the arguments outlined in Section 4. First, British Israelism and later Identity Christianity is best explained by the ultimate goal of religious and racial purity. These ideologies, drawn in part from a radical interpretation of Christian scriptures, create an argument for racial superiority, placing White Anglo-Saxon Christians at the top of its hierarchy and, by extension, justifying violent actions that have targeted Jews, blacks, and other nonwhites, with the ultimate goal of creating a "white nation." These groups have targeted citizens as well as the government to realize this goal. Identity Christians have also used apocalyptic thinking to call for the instigation of a race war, with the aim of ushering in a new salvific era marked by the "reestablishment" of white superiority on earth and the cleansing of what they believe to be Satan's offspring. Although spawning the creation of numerous groups, the strength of Identity Christian ideology and white supremacy lies in its ability to adapt and inspire new individuals and groups to act. This includes, more recently, the modification of the ideology to target a wider audience in the United States, particularly through the alt-right movement.

Buddhist Terrorism in Myanmar: The 969 Movement and Ma-Ba-Tha

Perhaps one of the most surprising manifestation of religiously motivated terrorism comes from Buddhist monks and activists in Myanmar. Beginning in 2012, two organizations comprised of Buddhist monks – the 969 Movement and Ma-Ba-Tha (the Association of Protection of Race and Religion) – formed and began to claim that Muslims in Myanmar were plotting to "Islamize" the country. Aided by a more open political environment and the proliferation of information technologies and social media, these groups have helped spark several anti-Muslim riots and terrorist acts throughout the country that have cost thousands of lives and, at its worst, have ideologically supported several waves of forced migration of Rohingya Muslims from Myanmar to neighboring countries; the most recent wave in 2017 produced "more than 655,000 refugees" (Amnesty International 2018, 270). What conditions have fueled the rise of Buddhist monks and the wider population calling for and using violence against Muslims in Myanmar, including terrorism and ethnic cleansing?

The history of Buddhism in Myanmar, and the pivotal role that Buddhist monks have played in the social and political life of the country, is important for understanding the conditions under which Buddhist activists have called for violence toward Muslims in Myanmar. More than 88 percent of the country is Buddhist and adheres to the Theravada tradition, a particular orientation of Buddhism that, historically, had strong ties between the monastic order (the Sangha) and political leadership. Myanmar had several dynasties and kingdoms in which the monastic order legitimated the leadership and the leadership, in return, supported the Sangha. This relationship between religious and political authority was severed in 1885, following Burma's defeat in the Third Anglo-Burmese war that sent the last king into exile and ended in the annexation of Burma to the British (Yegar 1972).

Despite the diminished political role of the Sangha, its influence on the population has remained strong through time. British scholar J. S. Furnivall (1956, 12) claims, "It is Buddhism that has molded social Burman life and thought and, to the present day, the ordinary Burman regards the terms

'Burman' and 'Buddhist' as practically equivalent and inseparable." Melford Sprio (1982, 396) argues, "There is probably no other clergy in the world which receives as much honour and respect as offered to the Buddhist monks of Burma." And Nyi Nyi Kyaw (2016, 187) asserts that "monks as guardians of Buddhism possess tremendous power in Myanmar society, which puts them more or less on par with official elites."

Modern Myanmar has attempted to limit the Sangha's participation in political life, but in practice, the Sangha has continued to play an important role in the bid for greater political participation and democratization. In 1936, the government forbid monks from voting or contesting elections (Kyaw 2016, 187). However, in 2007, monks played a critical role in the "Saffron Revolution," which paved the way for greater economic, social, and political liberalization in Myanmar (Kyaw 2016, 189). In fact, somewhat ironically, several argue that the current rise of anti-Muslim sentiment is connected to the bid for greater democratic liberties, including the right to vote and freedom of speech (Zin 2015, Kyaw 2016). Specifically, anti-Muslim rhetoric from monks has become a tool of popular mobilization, particularly conspiracy theories that the Muslims in Myanmar are plotting to undermine Myanmar's Buddhist culture through high birth rates, crime, and rape (Zin 2015). This narrative is built on a perceived history of Muslims in Myanmar and claims of their devious intentions.

In fact, the history of Muslims in Myanmar, and the government's treatment of this minority group, is a long and contested topic. Abdul Ghafur Hamid (2016) notes that most scholars agree that the presence of Muslims in Myanmar date back to the ninth century. Several waves of Muslims came to Myanmar since that time, including Muslims from Bengal at the end of the fifteenth century, who helped establish the Kingdom of Arakan, and even greater numbers of Indians, mostly Muslims, who came to Myanmar under British rule to be merchants and to serve other purposes. Yegar (2002) notes that, by the turn of the nineteenth century, there were twice as many Indian Muslims as local Muslims. "The influx of these immigrants (Hindu as well as Muslim) created a new minority which, from many standpoints, was larger and more highly developed, and certainly more alien and despised than certain groups" (2002, 28). Yegar goes on to describe that Indian Muslims, in particular, developed robust networks of social, economic, legal, and religious resources that allowed them to remain separate from their Buddhist counterparts (2002, 28). The influx of Indians under the British sparked several boycotts against Indian-run businesses (Kyaw 2016, 192) and fomented anti-Indian and anti-Muslim riots in 1930, 1931, and 1938 (Yegar 2002, 30).

Muslim communities in Myanmar also have a history of political mobilization and rebellion, particularly Rohingya Muslims, an ethnic minority who lives in Rakhine state, and whom Buddhist nationalists claim are not citizens of Myanmar but are Bangladeshis. Following the defeat of Japan in 1945, Muslim leaders in Rakine made a bid for autonomy from the rest of Burma. Rakine Muslims also formed a "mujahideen" insurgent movement in 1948 against the newly formed Burmese government, a movement that was eventually put down in 1961 (Yegar 2002, 37–47). A military coup in 1964 prompted greater controls over the population and an increase in discriminatory practices against minorities throughout the country, especially Muslims. Yegar (2002, 52) notes that between 1963 and 1967, an estimated 300,000 Indians left Myanmar, most of whom were Muslim. The Burmese government also began to restrict the rights of Rohingya Muslims in the country, eventually passing a citizenship law in 1982 that disenfranchised most of the ethnic minority and led to the revocation of their identity cards.

The Rohingya have faced several waves of forced migration at the hands of the government and military, including the creation of an estimated 22,000 refugees during World War II; a wave of more than 250,000 forced migrants from 1988 to 1992; and another wave beginning in 2012 of more than 168,000 Rohingya Muslims fleeing by boat and over land, in addition to tens of thousands seeking refuge within Myanmar as internally displaced people (Yegar 2002, 63–64; Tan 2017). The 2017 forced migration, the largest, followed on the heels of an August 25 attack by the newly rebranded insurgent group, the Arakan Rohingya Salvation Army, which targeted several police and military outposts in Rakhine, killing twelve security forces. In response, the military launched a massive clearing operation aimed at ridding the state of insurgents but, in practice, prompted the forced migration of at least 655,000 Rohingya (Amnesty International 2018, 270).

While these forced migrations have occurred largely at the hands of the Myanmar military and through government policy, Buddhist organizations, and popular sentiment in Myanmar more broadly, have painted these incidents as self-defense against a rising threat posed by Muslims in the country. Specifically, the narrative purports that the Buddhist majority in Myanmar is under attack from its Muslim minority and that Muslims aim to "deracinate" Myanmar through several means: marrying non-Muslim Burman women; polygamy; a high birthrate; conversion; and through economic means, including owning stores and restaurants (Kyaw 2016, 202–203).

Two groups in particular, the 969 Movement and Ma-Ba-Tha, have perpetuated this narrative and use their authority as Buddhist monks to communicate their message of hatred and fear to Myanmar's Buddhist majority. Founded in 2012, the 969 Movement derives its name from the numerical qualities of the Buddha (9), the Dhamma (6), and the Sangha (9), and is a counterpunch to Muslims' use of 786, which is a numerological reading of the Arabic letters that spell *Bismillah ir-Rahman ir-Rahim* (in the name of God, the most gracious, the most merciful), and which often hangs outside Muslim stores and homes (International Crisis Group 2017; Coclanis 2013, 26–27; Kyaw 2016, 196–199). Kyaw (2016, 185) argues that "the 969 campaign of Islamophobia invigorated a deeply held siege mentality with roots in colonial times. Its Buddhist audiences were made to believe that Buddhism and Buddhists in Myanmar ware under threat from Islam and Muslims in Myanmar and elsewhere." Coclanis (2013, 27) summarizes, "The main message of 969 was (and is) Burma for Buddhists, particularly for Buddhists who are Bamar rather than members of other ethnic groups." Kyaw (2016, 185) explains that the 969 Movement in particular uses videos and tapes that draw on well-known Buddhist formats to communicate its message: "969 propagandist monks sensationalize their sermons by stories of Buddhist women forcibly converted to Islam and often harassed by their Muslim husband, and by conspiracy theories of the Muslim plot to Islamize Myanmar."

Ma-Ba-Tha, which was founded in 2013 after the country's Buddhist Sangha Council banned the 969 Movement, has aimed to network Myanmar's 500,000 Buddhist monks in the pursuit of "defending Buddhism"

(International Crisis Group 2017, 11). In addition to spreading anti-Muslim rhetoric through its sermons, Ma-Ba-Tha has focused specifically the passage of four proposed laws: an interfaith marriage bill, the religious conversion bill; the monogamy bill; and the population control bill, all of which target Muslims in Myanmar and are intended to address the alleged threat posed by Muslim in the country (International Crisis Group 2017, 11–12). Kyaw (2016, 203) is quick to point out that a similar interfaith marriage law was attempted during colonial rule. Both the 969 Movement and Ma-Ba-Tha gained domestic and international attention through one of its members, Ashin Wirathu, a Buddhist monk who has been credited with helping to spread hatred toward Muslims throughout the country and who was imprisoned from 2003 to 2012 for inciting religious riots. In 2013, *Time* magazine called Wirathu "the face of Buddhist terror," and others have labeled him the "bin Laden" of Buddhism (Barron 2018).

Finally, these movements have spread their narrative through the proliferation of cell phones, the Internet, and social media. Robert Huish and Patrick Belaro (2018) note that access to the Internet and social media has become ubiquitous in the past eight years: "In 2010, Myanmar had 130,000 heavily restricted internet users. In seven years, SIM card prices plunged from more than US\$3,000 to \$1" (2018, 1). The authors go on to note that Facebook, in particular, had 30 million Burmese users by 2019 and "many of them view Facebook as the internet" (2018, 1). Zin (2015, 374) argues that this current wave of violence against Muslims "has now carried a new variable, which is undeterred propagation of hate speech coupled with clear political coordination." Zin goes on to argue, "Unlike under previous regimes, where anti-Muslim hate speech was either word-of-mouth propaganda manufactured by military intelligence officers or underground publications, people can now hear vitriolic attacks against Muslims in religious sermons from the intrusive loudspeakers of local monasteries or donation stations" (2015, 374). Zin further argues that "[p]eople encounter hate speech in books and handouts, watch it on DVDs that are conveniently available from sellers at almost every traffic junctions, and on social media" (2015, 374).

The increase in anti-Muslim rhetoric, proliferated by Buddhist monks, and the viral spread of these ideas through the internet and social media, have prompted several incidents of civilian-led violence against Muslims. In 2012, riots broke out between Buddhists and Muslims in the state of Rakhine, which left an estimated 200 dead and 140,000 displaced, most of whom were Muslims. That same year, in the city of Meiktilar, "Buddhist mobs destroyed Muslim neighborhoods, leaving at least 44 people dead, including 20 students and several teachers massacred at an Islamic school" (Zin 2015, 375). Zin (2015) in fact notes that, following the 2012 election campaign, which brought Ang San Suu Kyi's National Democratic Party to power, anti-Muslims riots increased exponentially. He suggests that political mobilization and increased access to the internet and social media, combined with new free speech laws, allowed anti-Muslim rhetoric to proliferate and inspire civilians to perpetrate acts of violence and terrorism against Muslim populations in Myanmar.

The rise of Buddhist organizations promoting anti-Muslim sentiment in Myanmar, their use of Buddhist narratives and networks, and the terror it has produced against the country's Muslim population can be explained by several of the causes of religious terrorism outlined in Section 4. First, the rise of Myanmar's Buddhist extremists conforms to the concepts of religious nationalism, especially the idea that the Buddhist faith and its people – Barmar Theravada Buddhists – are the rightful inhabitants of the country and therefore have the right to rule the country by Buddhist principles. Furthermore, these narratives claim that, despite being around 88 percent of the population, the Buddhist majority is under attack from the country's Muslim minority, an estimated six percent of the population, who aim to "Islamize" the country through interfaith and multiple marriages, high birth rates, conversion, and economic might. This narrative draws on a particular reading of history to bolster its argument, particularly the influx of Indian Muslims during British colonialism, and the contested history of Rohingya Muslims. Buddhist organizations, particularly the 969 Movement and Ma-Ba-Tha, have claimed to defend Myanmar's Buddhist majority by pressuring the government to enact laws that target the country's Muslim population, including excluding them from the most recent census, denying identity cards to its Rohingya Muslim population, and passing a series of laws designed to outlaw interfaith marriage and reduce birthrates within the country's Muslim population. Finally, Buddhist monks have drawn on several key resources to build and spread their argument, including the use of Buddhist sermons to make their case, and DVDs, books, pamphlets, and social media to disseminate their message. The result has been a series of deadly riots that have targeted individual Muslims and communities and – at its worst – these messages have aided military-led attacks against Rakhine Muslims that the UN Human Rights chief has called a "textbook example of ethnic cleansing" (UN News 2017).

The Jewish Defense League and Kahanism

In 1913, B'nai B'rith, a Jewish organization in the United States, launched the Anti-Defamation League "to stop, by appeals to reason and conscience and, if necessary, by appeals to law, the defamation of the Jewish people" (Anti-Defamation League 2019). While the ADL continued to work through the legal system to prosecute individuals discriminating against Jewish people, another group emerged in 1968, the Jewish Defense League, which claimed as its motto "never again" but, unlike the ADL, sought to defend Judaism by any means necessary, including violence. Prior to being banned in the United States in 2001, the JDL was responsible for several bombings, murder, assassination attempts, and acts of violence against African Americans in New York, Arab Americans, and targets connected to the Soviet Union. More broadly, its leader, Rabbi Meir Kahane, crafted an ideology calling for violence as a necessary means of defending the Jewish nation, earning him the nickname "Israel's Ayatollah" and even drawing comparisons to Hitler (Mergui and Simonnot 1987, 16). How did Kahane and the JDL come to see terrorism as the necessary path to defending the Jewish people?

The JDL was founded by Meir Kahane, an American from Brooklyn who earned a bachelor's degree in international relations, received training in law, and was an ordained Rabbi (Peri 2013). Prior to creating the JDL, Kahane was active in several right-wing Jewish organizations, including the paramilitary group Beitar, which was founded by the Jewish revolutionary Valdimir Jabotinsky (Peri 2013). At the age of fifteen, Kahane was arrested for taking part in a violent protest organized by Beitar (Dorman 2016, 418). In his thirties, Kahane became an informant for the FBI, adopting the name Michael King, and infiltrated the John Birch Society, which espoused anti-Semitic views in addition to attempting to subvert the US government (Mergui and Simonnot 1987, 16; Dorman 2016, 417).

Kahane believed that passivity had led to Jewish persecution and even the Holocaust; he thus stressed the need for a militant organization to combat what he saw as a lack of a Jewish response to anti-Semitism as well as a means of confronting Judaism's enemies (Dolgin 1977, 17–19). In his book explaining the reasons for creating the JDL, Kahane (1975, 5) writes: "The electrifying slogan "Never Again" was never meant to declare that a Holocaust would never occur again. . . . What "Never Again" always meant was quite another proposition. That as long as anyone attempted to repeat the Holocaust, never again would there be that same lack of reaction, that same indifference, that same fear. Never again would the JDL allow the Jewish Establishment to repeat its obscenity of World War II." In fact, he dedicated his 1975 book on the JDL to several "anti-heroes" – individuals and groups that he believed perpetuated Jewish passivity – including B'nai B'rith and the ADL.

Kahane further believed that violence was a necessary response to threats posed to Jewish communities everywhere and he "rejected the path of nonviolence as a symptom of historic oppression" (Dorman 2016, 427). Dorman (2016, 426) argues that "Kahane claimed that nonviolence came from Gandhi, Christianity and Quakerism, and therefore was culturally alien to a pre-exilic Jewish identity, which he associated with ancient Israelite feats at Masada, the Bar Kochba revolt, and Juddah Maccabee," referring to the Jewish-led revolts against the Roman and Seleucid Empires during Second Temple era Judaism. Afterman and Afterman (2015, 194) assert that Kahane drew on Biblical themes of the vengeance of God to call for action. "God is invoked as the 'God of revenge' and the eschatological future is conceived to be bound to the notion that Israel's redemption will culminate only once God has taken revenge upon Israel's enemies." And Pedazur and Perliger (2009, 74) argue, "Kahane opined that to harm a Jew was considered a desecration of God's name, thus making vengeance against the gentiles a religious precept." Juergensmeyer and Kitts (2011, 69) note that Kahane drew on apocalyptic themes to develop his theology, particularly "catastrophic messianism," which purports "the idea that the Messiah will come in a time of great conflict in which Jews triumph and praise God through their successes." Kahane himself proclaimed, "As far as I'm concerned, we are living the end of times. We are living a messianic era" (Mergui and Simonnot 1987, 44). This ideology of violence and revenge against Judaism's enemies became known as Kahanism.

In addition to its critique of existing Jewish organizations, the JDL had three broad enemies that it targeted. First, racial tensions in New York between African Americans and Jewish populations during the 1960s prompted the creation of "Jewish self-defense patrols" aimed at protecting Jewish communities in neighborhoods with shifting demographics (Mergui and Simonnot 1987, 16). These defense patrols morphed into the JDL in 1968, following a series of school strikes in the Brownsville area of Brooklyn that pitted African Americans against Jewish citizens over claims of persisting school segregation (Dorman 2016). Second, the JDL targeted the Soviet Union with the goal of pressuring it to allow its Jewish citizens to immigrate to Israel (Dolgin 1977). Within this objective, Mergui and Simonnot (1987, 16) note that the JDL aimed to spark a conflict between the United States and the Soviet Union so that, as Kahane put it, "'the problem of the Russian Jews becomes Nixon's problem.'" Joseph McCann (2006, 171) points out that the JDL "was the only group which deployed tactical violence on American soil in order to change the policy of a foreign entity." The JDL's third target was Arabs in the United States who it perceived to show aggression toward the state of Israel, particularly after the assassination of Jewish athletes at the 1972 Olympics in Munich. That same year, Kahane proclaimed: "There is only one solution to Arab terror – Jewish counter-terror" (Mergui and Simonnot 1987, 21).

Kahane constructed the JDL like a paramilitary organization, similar to Beitar. It set up a boot camp in upstate New York and put recruits through rigorous training in martial arts, marksmanship, and even bomb making (Mergui and Simonnot 1987, 16; Dolgin 1977, 32). It adopted as its flag the Star of David with a clenched fist in the middle, stressing its militant nature. Ironically, Dorman (2016) argues that Kahane also shaped the JDL after the Black Power movement and that the organization mimicked their slogans, including adapting the phrase "black is beautiful" to "Jewish is beautiful," referring to members of the JDL as "Jewish Panthers" and wearing black leather jackets and berets, similar to the Black Panthers. The JDL also mimicked the Black Power movement's principles, outlining five of its own: "Love of Israel and Judaism; Dignity and Pride; Iron Strength; Discipline and Unity; and Faith in the Indestructibility of the Jewish People" (Southern Poverty Law Center 2019b; Dorman 2016, 427). At its height, the JDL was believed to have 14,000 members throughout the United States, Canada, Britain, and the Netherlands (Mergui and Simonnot 1987, 17).

The JDL's operations ranged from harassment of its adversaries to assassination attempts to murder. The Southern Poverty Law Center (2019b) notes, "Throughout the 1970s and '80s, JDL members did everything from pouring blood over the head of a Soviet diplomat at a reception in Washington, D.C., to planting a smoke bomb in a Carnegie Hall performance of a Soviet orchestra. With each incident, the JDL claimed responsibility by phoning in its official slogan, in reference to the Holocaust, 'Never again!'" The JDL was even accused of attempting to create a radio-controlled plane that would deliver a bomb to the Soviet Embassy at the United Nations. This foiled attack was followed by several failed attempts to assassinate Soviet Ambassador Anantole Dobrynin, and in 1972, three JDL members were charged with murdering one individual after detonating a bomb but were later acquitted due to procedural problems with the investigation. In 1975, Kahane, who was now residing in Israel, served a one year sentence under house arrest in the United States following calls to assassinate Soviet diplomats and bomb the Iraqi Embassy (Mergui and Simonnot 1987, 18–22).

The overall Jewish response to Kahane and the JDL was anything but supportive. Mergui and Simonnot (1987, 16) describe that "[Kahane] aroused the hostility of the Jewish Community, who excluded him from their World Conference in Brussels in 1971." In Kahane's own writings, he describes the Jewish response to the JDL as a "fury," noting that organizations like the ADL and the National Jewish Community Relations Advisory Council went to various lengths to condemn the acts of the JDL, asking, "Is this any way for nice Jewish boys to behave?" Kahane claimed that this publicity only drew more recruits and money to his cause (1975, 98–99).

In 1971, Kahane immigrated to Israel and, in 1974, began a second organization, Kach ("Thus"), in addition to supporting the settler movement in the West Bank. Peri (2013) argues that, following Kahane's move to Israel, "his hostile attitude toward the 'other' – that is, US blacks – was now directed at Arabs in Israel." Kahane advocated for forcibly removing Palestinians and other non-Jews from Israel. When asked in an interview if he would drive Arabs in Israel out by force, Kahane answered: "The real problem is that I am not about to ask them to leave. I want to make them leave. I am saying to them that they must leave, and I'll make them leave" (Mergui and Simonnot 1987, 49–50). In 1984, Kahane's Kach party garnered enough votes to win one seat in the Knesset, Israel's parliament. Kahane's tenure in the Knesset was short-lived, however, and he was removed for espousing racist views. In 1990, Kahane was assassinated by an Arab assailant while giving a talk in New York City.

Kahane's ideology came to a shocking culmination in 1994, when Baruch Goldstein, a US-born medical doctor and former member of the JDL, stormed into the *Machpelah*, the Tomb of the Patriarchs in Hebron, and shot dead twenty-nine Palestinian Muslims in prayer before being beaten to death. Echoing Kahane's ideas, Goldstein's supporters claimed that he was doing what Israeli Defense Forces had failed to do, which is defend the Jewish people, and that he was enacting revenge for the 1929 massacre of Jewish settlers in the city by Muslims (Juergensmeyer 2000).

Kahane's ideology, his creation of the JDL, and its use of terrorism echo several of the broad arguments presented in Section 4. First, Kahane's ideology reflects fundamentalist thinking. As the group's name implies, the JDL saw their violent actions as a form of self-defense and preservation against Judaism's enemies, both external and internal. Kahane argued that a Jewish person under threat anywhere – Brooklyn, the Soviet Union, Israel – required immediate action to defend through all means necessary, including violence. Kahane further argued that working through the legal system, or attempting to preserve one's traditions, was not enough; responding to this threat required the use of violence. Within this line of reasoning, Kahane believed that Judaism was as much under threat from those within the faith as those attacking it, and the lack of a militant response created the conditions for a new Holocaust. Kahane also saw political activism as another means of realizing his vision, particularly his creation of Kach, a political party in Israel, and his time in the Knesset.

However, this was short-lived and unsuccessful. Finally, Kahane drew on apocalyptic expectations to build his case for using violence and terrorism against Judaism's adversaries, arguing that the world was in the end of times and that Jewish actions could hasten the coming of the messiah. Throughout, Kahane drew on historic Jewish examples of physical might and the use of force, such as the standoff at Masada, the Bar Kochba revolt, and Juddah Maccabee, along with more recent examples, including the revolutionary Jabotinsky and his militant organization Beitar, to build his ideology. He also drew from contemporary examples outside of Judaism, most notably the Black Power movement and the Black Panthers.

Importantly, Kahanism diverges from the theories of religiously motivated violence and terrorism outlined in Section 4. Specifically, Kahane's focus on revenge, on righting past wrongs both within Judaism and with Judaism's enemies, is not well-articulated in the four theories presented in Section 4. A "theology of revenge," as Afterman and Afterman call it, may be one of Kahane's lasting contributions to religiously motivated violence and terrorism and a grim mandate that may cross religious boundaries.

Aum Shinrikyo

Finally, it is important to consider religious groups that do not fit cleanly into one faith tradition but that have perpetrated acts of violence, including terrorism, as a means of furthering various goals. Academics tend to refer to these groups as "New Religious Movements" but they also go by a much more common title – cults. These groups often display behavior that is unique from and at tension with their mainstream religious counterparts, including individuals physically separating themselves from wider society, adopting distinct and extreme practices that demonstrate commitment, and displaying acute loyalty to the group (Iannaconne 1992).

Most New Religious Movements are not violent; however, those that do resort to violent behavior often turn their violence inward. This includes groups like the People's Temple Agricultural Project, more commonly known as "Jonestown," in which 912 people committed mass suicide in 1978 at the direction of Jim Jones, the group's leader (Maaga 1998). Another example is the Branch Davidians, a Texas-based group that believed Armageddon was near and began to stockpile weapons at the direction of its leader, David Koresh, which prompted an ATF raid in 1993. Following a fifty-one-day standoff between federal law enforcement agencies and the Davidans, the compound caught fire, killing seventy-six of its members (Wright 2011).

Although less common, New Religious Movements also turn their violence outward, and when they do so, this violence often takes the form of terrorism – targeting innocent civilians with a greater goal in mind. Exploring the relationship between New Religious Movements and terrorism is particularly important because, in addition to some of the spectacular and gruesome examples of violence these groups have perpetrated, at least two groups have used biological or chemical weapons to further their goals: the Rajneesh movement, which attempted to change elections in Oregon by poisoning salad bars with salmonella in 1984, sickening 751 people (Torok, et al 1997); and Aum Shinrikyo's attempt to deploy sarin gas on the Tokyo Subway on March 20, 1995, which killed 12 and injured thousands (and will be discussed further later). Although relatively few have resorted to terrorism, New Religious Movements have shown their willingness to use WMD, making them a particularly important type of religious terrorism to investigate.

Aum Shinrikyo was founded by Chizu Matsumo, a semiblind Japanese national who claimed to have achieved enlightenment while visiting the Himalayas in 1986. He changed his name to Shoko Asahara ("the Holy") and started a meditation center in Tokyo that became Aum Shinrikyo ("the supreme truth"; Juergensmeyer 2000, 107). Asahara drew from a mixture of religious traditions to build his faith system, including Buddhism, Hinduism, Taoism, the predictions of Nostradamus, and even aspects of Christianity (Reader 1996). Asahara preached that salvation from the ills of society was possible by joining Aum, purchasing its literature, attending various sessions, and pledging loyalty to his leadership. Over time, Asahara's message took on a more apocalyptic tone, claiming that Japanese society was under threat from the United States, which aimed to destroy the country through a nuclear or chemical attack. Only those who followed Asahara's teaching and achieved a degree of enlightenment would be spared and reincarnated to repopulate the earth. Robert Jay Lifton (2000, 8) asserts, "No truth was more central to Aum than the principle that world salvation could be achieved only by bringing about the deaths of just about everyone on this earth." Ian Reader (1996, 2) summarizes that Shoko Asahara "proclaimed that he was a messiah who had come to save his followers from the apocalypse and lead them forward to form a new, ideal spiritual universe that would emerge from the ruins of the old." This apocalyptic message, paradoxically, led Asahara to pursue chemical and biological weapons aimed at fomenting the apocalypse and cleansing the world of evil.

Asahara himself is important for understanding the rise of Aum Shinrikyo and, in fact, Reader (1996, 12) claims, "Aum Shinrikyo's development is so closely interwoven with the life and utterances of its leader Asahara Shoko that the two cannot be separated." Asahara suffered from a childhood bout of glaucoma that left him partially blind and required him to attend a special school. At this school, he reportedly ruled over his completely blind classmates. As Robins and Post (1997, 33) put it, "In the land of the blind, the one-eyed man is king." He showed signs of narcissism and allegedly bragged to his fellow students that he would run for office and someday become Japan's prime minister. Parachini (2005, 17) summarizes Asahara by claiming: "He was charismatic, had delusions of grandeur, and was paranoid. These personality traits combined to make him a domineering and controlling leader. He was the guru, and group members were devoted to him above all else." Parachini further notes: "Aum's highly centralized structure and highly disciplined nature allowed it to pursue certain objectives with intense focus. The strength of this focused determination also served to foster an 'echo chamber' effect in the organization. No matter how evil and self-destructive Asahara's command or the command of one of his close associates, Aum members obeyed" (2005, 17).

Shoko Asahara targeted disaffected middle-class individuals to join his group – those who had achieved a level of success and yet were lonely, unfulfilled, or exhausted. Sullivan (2011, 2) notes, "Teenagers and students made up a considerable portion of the cult's membership, some of them brilliant graduates of Japan's top universities, with advanced degrees in medicine, law, and science." Somewhat unusual for cults, which usually rely on direct contact between the leader and follower, Aum was able to establish personal connections through literature and even by selling vials of his blood and hair, allowing Aum to expand beyond Japan and to begin chapters in the United States, Germany, Sri Lanka, Taiwan, and Russia (Parachini 2005). By the time of the subway attack, Aum was believed to have around 10,000 Japanese members, 30,000 followers in Russia, and unknown numbers elsewhere (Reader 1996, 1; Robins and Post 1997, 133).

Aum was also widely criticized for using a variety of hostile and coercive techniques aimed at keeping members in its organization and punishing those who attempted to leave. In 1988, a pledge member died as part of an initiation ritual, raising suspicions about the group and its tactics. In 1989, another member was killed after trying to leave the organization (Parachini 2005, 13). Following these incidents, Aum was tied to the murder of human rights lawyer Tsutsumi Sakamoto, his wife, and their fourteen-month-old son, after he defended Aum members who wanted to be released from the group (Parachini 2005).

Shoko Ashara had several earthly and eternal goals for Aum Shinrikyo and its followers. From the beginning, a key objective of his religious movement appeared to be financial. Aum created a number of legitimate and illegitimate sources of revenue, including membership fees, Aum-related literature, noodle shops, illegal drugs, software manufacturing, and even bribes from local officials to prevent Aum from setting up chapters in their districts (Simons 2006). One estimate put Aum's worth at "between $300 million and $1 billion" by the time of the attack (Robins and Post 1997, 135); another estimate put the number at $1.5 billion by 1995 (Sullivan 2011).

Asahara and his followers also had political goals. In 1989, Asahara and twenty-four other members of Aum ran for seats in the Japanese parliament. Simons (2006, 39) writes, "These Aum political candidates thought that by gaining seats on various political agencies they would be able to publicize the group and Asahara's teachings and thereby provide salvation to more people." However, Ashara and the other Aum candidates were unable to gain significant votes and were soundly defeated.

Following his failed attempt at being elected to parliament, Ashara began to preach more about his apocalyptic expectations. Parachini (2005,

14) argues: "His sense of alienation and rejection increased dramatically following the election. The group's problems were compounded by a decrease in the number of new members and an increase in the number of members who sought to leave. Asahara's rhetoric became increasingly apocalyptic and violent. In many ways, the events of this period established the ideological justification for Aum's increasingly confrontational stance and its robust weapons development and procurement programs."

Specifically, Asahara's apocalyptic narrative purported that a nuclear holocaust was on the horizon, but that those who followed his teachings would be saved and "that even nuclear war would not be a problem for his believers because an emancipated person may be born into this world again with a new physical body" (Robins and Post 1997, 131). Asharah planned to use chemical and biological weapons and blame the attack on the United States, which it claimed had designs to take over Japan. This initial attack would, in turn, spark World War III, the destruction of the planet, and its ultimate salvation through the reincarnation of the faithful to repopulate the earth.

Aum Shinrikyo began to develop biological and chemical weapons capabilities with the aim of fomenting this apocalyptic scenario. Sullivan (2011, 2) reports that "by mid-1993 Aum had constructed a plant to manufacture automatic weapons, as well as crude but operational chemical and biological weapons facilities, where it was able to produce botulism toxin, anthrax bacteria, sarin gas, and hydrogen cyanide." Olson (1999, 154) writes that "Aum dabbled in many different biological agents. They cultured and experimented with botulin toxin, anthrax, cholera, and Q fever" and even Ebola. Lifton (2000, 205) asserts that "ultimate weapons in general became bound up with his action prophecy in pressing towards Armageddon."

Aum attempted several biological and chemical attacks prior to the 1995 sarin attack on the Tokyo subway. Olson (1999, 514) chronicles an April 1990 attempt to release botulin toxin near the Diet in Tokyo, another attempt to disperse botulin in 1993 during the wedding of the crown prince, a failed attempt to release anthrax from its office building in Tokyo, and one more attempt to spray botulin in 1995, just before the sarin attack on the subway. Olson surmises that these attacks may not have succeeded for a few reasons: "The cult may not have had the right agents or the right technologic facilities; they could have overcooked the bioagents or not known how to use them," and "while the cult was well financed, it was not very successful in its efforts to recruit biological scientists" (1999, 514).

Asahara's apocalyptic imagination eventually led to Aum's 1995 sarin gas attack on the Tokyo subway, which killed twelve and wounded thousands. The attack itself did not go according to plan, and the perpetrators failed to properly deploy the weapons, which could have killed upwards of twenty thousand people, had they been properly ignited (Robins and Post 1997). Following the attack, investigations uncovered extensive weapons depots, chemical and biological factories, and considerable cash, indicating that Aum intended to carry out future deadly attacks (Robins and Post 1997). Asahara and his top lieutenants were arrested, along with the perpetrators of the attack. Asahara was executed in 2018.

The rise of Aum Shinrikyo and its ultimate aim of deploying WMD to ignite the apocalypse and repopulate the world with its faithful followers is a clear example of fomenting the apocalypse as a paradoxical means of saving the earth. Ashara's teachings claimed that nuclear war was imminent and that only through his teachings could individuals be saved from the horrors of nuclear holocaust and reborn into a new and purified world. Ashahara's message, therefore, was one of eternal salvation from the suffering and darkest creations of this world. Robins and Post (1997) note that this message of apocalyptic salvation gained traction through the dysfunctional dynamic between Asahara, the psychologically wounded leader, and his needy followers, who together formed a "lock and key" relationship that allowed for the perpetuation of radical ideas. Shoko Asahara displayed traits of narcissism, paranoia, and cruelty from an early age, along with the desire to be a great leader and figure of importance. Asahara's focus on individuals who were successful, but had become disaffected and disillusioned by their middle-class lives, conforms to the idea of a "cognitive opening" described by Wictorowicz (2005), which paved the way for "religious seeking." Asharaha was able to provide a belief system that explained the personal suffering of these individuals and their path to liberation, both in this world and the next. At its most extreme, this "lock and key relationship" between Asahara and his followers allowed for the unthinkable to occur – the creation and deployment of a chemical weapon to potentially kill tens of thousands-of people.

Conclusion

The brief overview of these five case studies reveals several conditions under which groups use religious resources to perpetrate acts of terrorism. First, each of the cases describes a perceived threat posed by factors external to the faith, and the need to remove that sense of threat, as justification for terrorist acts. In Myanmar, the annexation of the country to the British in 1885, followed by the influx of Indian Muslims to the country, prompted claims that Muslims were attempting to take over the country and destroy the Buddhist nature of its people, sparking a series of protests and riots. This narrative of Muslims attempting to "Islamize" the country helped inform later claims that all Muslims are a threat to Myanmar, despite being around only 6 percent of the population, and paved the way for acts of terrorism against Muslims throughout the country and the mass expulsion of Rohingya in 2012 and 2017. In the United States, Identity Christianity purports that white Anglo-Saxons are under threat from Jews, who have taken control of financial systems and the government, and people of color, who are the offspring of Satan. Only a race war will purify the land and prevent a "white genocide." Kahanism claims that Jews are under perpetual attack, as evidenced by history, and that it is necessary to defend against these threats "by any means necessary," including violence. Even ISIL claims that the rise of the secular state, a Western concept, is threatening Islam around the world.

As importantly, these cases show an acute sense of threat by those within the faith as well. ISIL purports that Shia Muslims, Sufis, and secular Sunnis have corrupted the true path of Islam, and only by the cleansing the world of these Muslim apostates can Islam be rightly restored. The JDL leveled scathing critiques against mainstream Jewish organizations, such as the ADL, claiming that their nonviolent response was paving the way for another holocaust. And white supremacists claim to have the true understanding of scripture and through social media, preaching and acts of terrorism, aim to awaken misguided (white) Christians to their true identities, in addition to attacking enemies outside the faith.

Second, several of these groups have drawn from the "cognitive openings" that real-life circumstances create in vulnerable populations to offer a solution through "religious seeking" and the call to violent action against civilians. ISIL, for example, names foreign policy injustices, the rise of secular society, and the perversion of Islam as threats demanding a response from Muslims around the globe. As importantly, they offer a path for addressing these grievances; they provide instruction for how to live a righteous life, a community of support for living that life, and the chance to change their communities and even the world. They offer purpose and hope for the disenfranchised, as well as violent revenge for those that have wronged them or their community. White supremacists provide a similar program to ISIL. And Aum Shinrikyo spoke to disillusioned middle-class individuals who had achieved success and yet were still unfulfilled, offering them hope and direction. These promises of redemption, revenge, and salvation created the impetus for violence against otherwise innocent civilians.

Third, these cases reveal that groups use religious resources in several ways to further their cause. Perhaps most critical, these groups draw from religious history, symbols, and scripture to create an interpretation of the faith that calls for and justifies specific acts of violence, ranging from purifying the faith (ISIL and white supremacists) to creating religious nations (Buddhists in Myanmar, white supremacists, and ISIL) to standing up governments (ISIL and white supremacists) to hastening the apocalypse (Aum Shinrikyo, Kahanism, ISIL, and white supremacists). Religious leaders are another important resource that offers direction and legitimacy to these groups. The sources of religious authority are typically self-appointed, in the case of Shoko Asahara and most white supremacists, but some are bona fide religious leaders as well, including Buddhist monks in Myanmar, Rabbi Kahane of the JDL, and al-Baghdadi's credentials as a religious scholar in Sunni Islam. Finally, most of these radical groups often make use of preexisting networks to spread their cause and gain recruits, including networks of monks in Myanmar, preexisting and like-minded Jewish organizations, like Beitar, for the JDL, and radical Salafi groups that have pledged allegiance to ISIL. In the cases of white supremacy and Aum Shinrikyo, these movements were forced to build networks from scratch, which, in the case of white supremacists, may have slowed the spread of the movement down considerably.

The cases also show how various interpretations of faiths are recycled and adapted over time. ISIL's ideology builds on preexisting themes of apocalypticism, defense of faith, and the example of the Prophet – themes that are familiar to most Muslims – but adapts them to present-day circumstances to justify violent actions. In this case, ISIL's recycling of ideas has led to more extreme understandings of the faith. Identity Christianity in the United States, by contrast, appears to be recycling ideas that link white supremacy to faith with the aim of softening these ideas and diffusing them into mainstream social and political discourse. In almost all of the cases, Aum Shinrikyo perhaps being the exception, these groups have built on preexisting interpretations of the faith, capitalizing on ideas that have already been circulated throughout various communities, and may resonate with some adherents.

Finally, the JDL presents an interesting finding of how religion has been used to justify terrorism, a "theology of revenge" as Afterman and Afterman (2015) call it. The authors argue that Meir Kahane developed an understanding of Judaism that not only justifies violence but demands it based on avenging violence done against fellow members of the Jewish nation. This theology of revenge justified acts of terrorism against Soviet targets in the United States, and the 1994 murder of twenty-nine Muslims in Hebron as revenge for the 1929 massacre of Jews in the same city.

6 Countering Religious Terrorism

The many examples of religious terrorism across time and tradition, its apparent growth in recent decades, and the potential for its increasing lethality raise questions about how to counter this threat. Recent approaches to countering religious terrorism have taken three broad trajectories. First, at the state level, countries have stepped up "homeland security," including "hardening" potential targets like airports and government buildings, restricting access to materials that could be used to perpetrate acts of terrorism, and even imposing emergency measures that may restrict some civil liberties. For example, the US Congress created the Patriot Act after 9/11, which increased funds for counterterrorism efforts, granted broader authorities for law enforcement surveillance, and allowed the use of military force to counter terrorist threats abroad (H.R. 3162 2001). Similarly, the French government declared a state of emergency following the November 2015 terrorist attacks in Paris, which included expanding law enforcement's ability to detain individuals and property, blocking websites inciting acts of terrorism, restricting public assemblies, and creating "security zones" that limited the public's freedom of movement (Gouvernment.fr 2015). Governments have taken these measures largely after terrorist attacks, with the aim of making future terrorist acts more difficult to execute. Homeland security, in other words, focuses on countering acts of terrorism irrespective of terrorists' motives; it is not specific to religious terrorism.

Second, at the state and international levels, governments and coalitions have targeted specific groups and individuals accused of perpetrating acts of terrorism. At the state level, these measures have included surveilling individuals and groups believed to have terrorist intentions and using various domestic law enforcement agencies to apprehend and try these individuals in a court of law. At the international level, coalitions of militaries have attempted to break up terrorist organizations and networks through intelligence gathering, killing or capturing key individuals, and denying territory and resources necessary for groups to plan and train for terrorist acts. Counterterrorism operations have ranged from covert operations, including US Operation "Neptune Spear," which killed Bin Laden in 2011, to drone strikes, like the one that killed US-born radical Anwar al-Awlaki in Yemen in 2001, to direct military confrontation, such as Operation Enduring Freedom, a NATO-led effort that targeted terrorists in Afghanistan. As with homeland security, this approach does not specifically address religious terrorism, although the main targets of these current multistate efforts are groups tied to radical and violent interpretations of Islam.

Third, counterterrorism efforts have attempted to challenge the underlying ideas and conditions motivating terrorist acts – what is broadly known as countering violent extremism (CVE). These efforts take three broad trajectories: "disengagement" and "deradicalization programs," designed to separate individuals from terrorist groups and rehabilitate those who have already become radicalized; "counter-radicalization," which aim to address vulnerable populations particularly susceptible to radicalization; and "anti-radicalization programs," which aim to prevent the general population from becoming radicalized in the first place (Horgan 2009; Clutterbuck 2015). These initiatives have focused heavily on countering radical interpretations of Islam; however, the underlying logic behind these approaches could easily apply to other radical understandings of faith systems as well. Each of these CVE programs is explored further in the following subsections.

Disengagement and Deradicalization Programs

Disengagement and deradicalizations programs aim to separate individuals from terrorist groups or networks and rehabilitate those who have already become radicalized. Lawrence Rubin (2011, 27) defines disengagement as "the behavioral change away from involvement with terrorist groups and activities that may or may not accompany an ideological change." Lindsay Clutterbuck (2015, 1) argues that the term deradicalization "should only be used to refer to the methods and techniques used to undermine and reverse the completed radicalization process, thereby reducing the potential risk to society from terrorism." And John Horgan (2009, 153) defines deradicalization as "the social and psychological process whereby an individual's commitment to, and involvement in, violent radicalization is reduced to the extent that they are no longer at risk of involvement and engagement in violent activity."

One of the main ways by which individuals are disengaged from terrorist groups and deradicalized is through arrest and incarceration for collaborating with nefarious groups, attempting to perpetrate terrorist acts, or successfully executing these acts. Perhaps one of the first prison-based deradicalization programs began in Algeria in the 1990s, during its crisis with the Armed Islamic Group (GIA) and the Islamic Salvation Army (Ashour 2011). Around the same time, Egypt began its own deradicalization program, which took on increased importance after the radical Islamist group *Gaamat al-Islamiyyah* murdered sixty-two tourists visiting the historic site of Luxor in 1997 (Rubin 2011). Despite being deemed initially unsuccessful, Gaamat's leadership began to renounce violence around the year 2000 in written tracts and through dialogue with their imprisoned rank and file. In 2007, the Egyptian Islamic Jihad also renounced violence (Ashour 2011). Following 9/11, several countries experimented with their own deradicalization programs for incarcerated terrorists, including Saudi Arabia, Singapore, Yemen, and even in US detention centers in Iraq (Boucek 2011; Gunaratna and Bin Mohamed Hassan 2011; Al-Hitar 2011; Stone 2011).

Deradicalization efforts in prisons have focused on several specific initiatives aimed at reeducating radicalized individuals and preparing them to be productive members of society. One of the key efforts across various programs has been religious education. These programs work under the assumption that individuals are not well informed of their religion's scriptures, doctrines, or traditions, allowing extremists to claim that their interpretations are legitimate. In Singapore, for example, the government created the Religious Rehabilitation Group, compiled of Muslim clerics, to provide religious education to detainees and specifically target and undermine the ideological points emphasized by violent extremist groups (Gunaratna and Bin Mohamed Hassan 2011). Egypt and Saudi Arabia also have focused on religious reeducation as part of their deradicalizaton programs (Rubin 2011; Boucek 2011).

Governments also initiated dialogue programs with violent extremist groups as a means of deradicalization. Both Algeria's and Egypt's governments worked through the Muslim Brotherhood to develop dialogues with incarcerated leaders of extremists groups, aimed at addressing some of their grievances and encouraging leaders and their followers to abandon violence (Ashour 2011; Rubin 2011). Saudi Arabia developed a Religious Subcommittee through its Ministry of Interior that brought together 150 Islamic scholars and academics who engaged in dialogue with prisoners (Boucek 2011, 78). Beginning in 2002, Yemen focused heavily on a dialogue-based deradicalization program, or *hiwar* in Arabic, emphasizing key principles in Islam as a foundation for discussions between the government and terrorist groups. The government convened four phases of the dialogue, from 2002 to 2004, which included a mixture of incarcerated individuals and those with suspected ties to terrorist groups. Individuals who renounced violence and their past as un-Islamic, both in writing and by swearing to God, were given presidential pardons and released (Al-Hitar 2011, 118–119). In addition to this series of direct dialogues, the government also created "indirect" dialogues between religious scholars and terrorists via media sources to "strengthen the correct conceptions of Islam and to refute the flawed concepts pertaining to the issues that have been identified as the themes of the dialogue" (Al-Hitar 2011, 111). At the time, the dialogues were deemed a success; however, Yemen has since seen a resurgent in terrorist activity, both from Al-Qaeda in the Arabian Peninsula and ISIL, in addition to its persisting civil war.

Governments also created programs aimed at deradicalization through the internet and social media. As part of its "PRAC" strategy (prevention, rehabilitation, and aftercare), Saudi Arabia developed an online presence called the "Tranquility Campaign," designed to counter sites run by al-Qaeda and similar groups. Specifically, a nongovernmental organization studied online chat rooms and other social media sources to actively engage in dialogue with radicalized individuals via the Internet. Abdulrahman Al-Hadlaq (2011, 62) notes that this effort was so successful that al-Qaeda "issued statements to its followers warning them to refrain from engaging with members of the Tranquility Campaign, an indication of its positive impact on radicals and sympathizers."

Several deradicalization programs also focused on addressing the longer-term need for rehabilitation. Saudi Arabia developed perhaps the most comprehensive long-term strategy that includes providing psychological counseling, offering art therapy, evaluating an individual's "social status," engaging family members, providing vocational training, and even helping to pay for wedding expenses (Boucek 2011). In Singapore, the government created the Community Engagement Programme (CEP) to address long-term issues facing radicalized individuals and vulnerable populations through a "bottom-up" approach that gave ownership of the process to local communities. The CEP brings together a variety of resources that aim to rehabilitate affected individuals, including social, economic, and psychological resources (Gunaratna and Bin Mohamed Hassan 2011).

Separate from programs aimed at specifically deradicalizating Muslims, organizations in Europe and the United States also created several "exit" programs for white supremacists beginning in the 1990s, including programs in Sweden and Germany (Lenz 2016). In the United States, former white supremacists launched a nonprofit called "Life after Hate" in 2011, with the goal of deradicalizing white supremacists through several initiatives, including "Formers Anonymous," a twelve-step recovery program; "ExitUSA," which focuses on disengaging white supremacists and creating long-term rehabilitation strategies; and an online presence that directly trolls and targets hate speech through #WeCounterHate (Lentz 2016).

Counter-Radicalization Programs

Whereas deradicalization programs target individuals that have already become radicalized and most likely have contributed to or committed acts of violence, counter-radicalization programs focus on deterring at-risk populations from becoming fully radicalized. Experts have identified several types of communities that are particularly vulnerable for radicalization. First, internally displaced individuals and refugees may be susceptible to radicalization. A 2015 RAND study, for example, notes that the wars in Iraq and Syria have produced more than four million refugees, and, as Section 4 discussed, more than a million Rohingya Muslims have been displaced from Myanmar in recent years, possibly making these groups vulnerable to radicalization. The authors argue that refugees are at greater risk of radicalization with "the geographic placement and legal status of the refugees, the level of social and economic support for local populations in those locations, the preexistence of militant groups in refugee areas, and – perhaps more critical – the policies and actions of the receiving country, including its acceptance of militant organizations and its ability to provide security" (Sude, Stebbins, and Weilant 2015, 2). The report advocates for a mixture of host-country policies to improve living conditions as possible mitigation strategies for radicalization: allow refugees greater employment opportunities, particularly youth; tighten camp security; improve opportunities for education; and increase donations from foreign countries to help refugees.

Another at-risk population for radicalization is immigrant communities. In Europe and North America, governments have paid considerable attention to first- and second-generation immigrant communities that are believed to be vulnerable to radicalization. Great Britain's "Prevent" program, for example, has focused on preventative strategies to address radicalization by gaining a greater understanding of the social, political, and economic grievances migrant communities face and addressing those needs (QIASS 2012). Brown and Saeed (2014) are quick to point out that lack of economic opportunity and isolation from the wider population are not the only spaces where individuals can become radicalized; universities are also places where young, intelligent, and idealistic individuals are vulnerable to radical ideas and require their own counter-radicalization strategies.

Several programs focus on reducing radicalization within these vulnerable populations. A key approach has been empowering local communities to address vulnerabilities themselves. For example, in 2004, the Dutch government developed a counter-radicalization plan aimed at addressing not only violent radicalism but also nonviolent radicalism that challenges democratic principles and the integration of immigrant communities into wider society. The government pushed the program down to the local level "because the Dutch government believes that local authorities are in a better position to detect problems and implement solutions" (Vidino 2008, 12). Some of the programs implemented include dialogues, festivals, engagement programs for women, and overall efforts to build relationships between Dutch and immigrant communities. Lorenzo Vindino (2008, 13) concludes, "Most of the programs seem to focus on the concept of empowering the individual and making him or her feel part of society."

Singapore also has focused heavily on a community approach to counter-radicalization through its "Community Engagement Programme," which aims to "give local ownership" and target vulnerable populations that might become radicalized due to the spread of extreme ideologies propagated by al-Qaeda and its local affiliates. The program provides local leaders with knowledge on identifying radicalism, resources for addressing these dangers, and tools for mitigating inter-ethnic conflict after incidents (Gunaratna and Mohamed Hassan 2011).

In the United States, several city governments have initiated community-based programs aimed at counter-radicalization. The City of Los Angeles, for example, began to develop a CVE program in 2008 that was designed to address countering extreme ideologies broadly and radical Islamic ideas specifically. The program focuses on three "pillars" at the local level: prevention of radicalization, intervention in cases where radicalization may be occurring, and interdiction where radicalization is known to be occurring. The city's CVE program has worked through its Human Relations Commission to bring together law enforcement, academics, NGOs, and community activists, with the aim of building relationships with stakeholders in the city and developing a comprehensive, community-based approach to counter-radicalization (City of Los Angeles 2015).

Several NGOs and nonprofit organizations have also worked to help at-risk communities develop resources aimed at identifying and addressing the threat of radicalization. In the United States, the Muslim Political Affairs Committee (MPAC), a nonprofit located in Washington, DC, and Los Angeles, developed a document titled "Safe Spaces: A Toolkit for Empowering Communities and Addressing Ideological Violence," which aims to be "a practical resource to help deal with the possibility of seemingly minor but troubling incidents of extremism and violence" for communities (MPAC 2015, 7). Some of the topics discussed include "Recommended actions for mosques and other faith-based community institutions," "What an intervention can look like – some basic principles," and "Building relationships with your local law enforcement agencies" (MPAC 2015, 3). The document is available for free online.

Anti-Radicalization Programs

Anti-radicalization programs take the broadest approach to addressing the threat posed by violent extremism by aiming to inoculate the general population from extreme ideas and behavior before individuals and groups become vulnerable to these ideas. These programs tend to focus heavily on education as a means of exposing individuals to diversity, developing tolerance, and fostering critical thinking skills. For example, several countries have initiated public service campaigns aimed at raising awareness of extremism and encouraging greater tolerance. Saudi Arabia created a public information and communication program to "foster cooperation between the state and the public; highlight damage done by terrorism and extremism; and end public support for and tolerance for extremist beliefs" (Boucek 2011, 77). In Singapore, academics and communities of interest have developed websites and blogs designed to challenge extreme interpretations of the faith, provide alternate and tolerant interpretations, and educate non-Muslims on the faith to combat Islamaphobia. Experts have also written and provided booklets free of charge that challenge extremist ideas and offer alternative interpretations of texts and practices (Gunaratna and Mohamed Hassan 2011, 53).

Governments and NGOs also have introduced anti-radicalization programs in school systems that focus on religious tolerance, empathy, and critical-thinking skills. Following the 2002 Bali bombings in Indonesia, neighboring Australia introduced the "Beyond Bali Education Program," a collaboration between Curtin University, the Bali Peace Park Association, and the Australian government. This program aims to teach critical-thinking skills, expose students to diversity, and introduce nonviolent conflict resolution skills in public and private schools, including religious schools (Aly, Taylor, and Karnovsky 2014). Saudi Arabia has created prevention programs for its school system that range from classes to distributing books and pamphlets to writing and art contests. In addition to educating children on the dangers of extremism, these programs also aim to educate students' parents on these issues (Boucek 2011, 75–76). And Singapore has focused heavily on engaging and educating youth on the dangers of extremism through a variety of programs (Mohammad Hassan and Gunaratna 2011, 52).

Countries also have created "national dialogues," with the aim of protecting the population against extremist ideas. Yemen, as mentioned, developed a media-based dialogue program that aimed to educate the entire population (Al-Hitar 2011). Saudi Arabia established the King Abdul Aziz Center for National Dialogue in 2003 to "combat extremism and promote moderate culture among various sections of society" (Al-Hadlaq 2011, 63). In Qatar, the government created the Doha Debates in 2004, with the aim of bringing together panels of experts on various topics, including extremism, to highlight the importance of logic and evidence-based debate on controversial topics. These debates are available online; they have partnered with TED Talks, Fortify Rights (a nonprofit human rights group in Southeast Asia), and Vox Media. They also are broadcast on Al Jazeera around the world (Doha Debates 2019).

In the United Kingdom, the Quilliam Foundation was founded in 2008 as "the world's first counter-extremism organization" (Quilliam Foundation 2019). The foundation calls on governments, academics, community activists, and others to create "a full spectrum and values-based approach to counter-extremism which means promoting pluralism and inspiring change." Quilliam produces reports and other publications, in addition to offering workshops, education, dialogues, and other outreach programs designed to "generate creative, informed and inclusive discussions to counter the ideological underpinnings of terrorism, while simultaneously providing evidence-based policy recommendations to governments, and building civil society networks and programmes to lead the change towards a more positive future" (Quilliam Foundation 2019).

Deradicalization, counter-radicalization, and anti-radicalization programs face several challenges along the road to successful implementation. First, governments need to have the political will to create these programs in the first place and recognize that police and military actions alone are unlikely to eradicate these groups and, in some cases, may be feeding their narratives of oppression. In most cases, creating programs aimed at reducing religiously motivated terrorism requires acknowledging that there are grievances that undergird calls for violence. Virtually all of the deradicalization programs described herein required governments to both acknowledge the existence of groups and individuals perpetrating acts of terrorism and to consider that they may need to change policies, address issues of social and economic marginalization, and introduce education initiatives in order to undercut the messages of extremists.

In the case of deradicalization programs specifically, most of these efforts directly engage criminals who have collaborated with known terrorists or perpetrated terrorist acts themselves. In many cases, therefore, these programs require some form of amnesty for criminals willing to renounce violence and change their ways; however, whom to release and under what conditions is difficult to determine. For example, by 2002, the Egyptian government claimed to have released between 15,000 and 20,000 Gamaat members that had renounced violent jihad and that did not have blood on their hands (Rubin 2011, 31). Algeria also created an extensive amnesty program for members of the Islamic Salvation Front and GIA, releasing "tens of thousands of political prisoners" between 1999 and 2005, including "high-profile" leaders like Ali Belhaj, the founder of GIA (Ashour 2011, 19). The Yemeni government granted presidential pardons to individuals who participated in deradicalization dialogues between 2002 and 2005, and who signed an agreement and swore to God that they would renounce all forms of violence (Al-Hitar 2011, 118–120). These programs require not only creating legal space for the forgiveness and release of violent criminals but also preparing communities to take back these individuals. This may not be easy if these groups have perpetrated considerable violence against the population.

Second, programs aimed at undercutting religious extremism and terrorism require the right "messenger" – the right intermediaries – that can navigate between the government and the terrorists to negotiate and effect change. In Egypt and Algeria, the governments turned to the Muslim Brotherhood for help with reaching out to terrorist groups. Singapore turned to its council of Muslim scholars to help identify the underlying problems that were allowing terrorist groups to radicalize individuals. And the Quillium Foundation and Life after Hate were created by former radicalized individuals who could act as intermediaries and develop programs aimed at deradicalization and counter-radicalization.

Finally, CVE programs require considerable resources. Perhaps most critically, these programs require substantial financial resources. The programs in Saudi Arabia and Singapore include a wide array of programs that are undoubtedly expensive, including establishing long-term rehabilitation programs, developing curricula, running youth programs, and creating public media campaigns. Governments and populations need the political will to devote funds to these programs, in addition to having sufficient capital to allocate to deradicalization, counter-radicalization, and anti-radicalization programs. These programs also require considerable man-power to provide education, provide counseling services, and monitor individuals who have been released from detention. Not all countries have these resources at their disposal – particularly countries that have been through decades of war and instability.

Conclusion

Religiously motivated violence and terrorism is not a new phenomenon, nor is it confined to one faith tradition. Moreover, acts of terrorism done in the name of faith are unlikely to go away. In fact, religiously motivated terrorism may be on the rise and become more deadly as groups develop and deploy more lethal forms of violence to further their goals. Therefore, better understanding the conditions under which individuals and groups call for violence in the name of faith is imperative, as is devising effective policies aimed at countering these groups.

This brief introduction to the topic has aimed to provide insights into the causes of religiously motivated terrorism by, first, providing an overview of what terrorism is and offering a broad discussion on religion, including beliefs, practices, and resources that could be used to motivate and justify violence. It then summarized four broad arguments for the conditions under which religious violence occurs: fundamentalist calls for purity, religious nationalists' aim to seize the state, groups wishing to foment the apocalypse, and the conditions under which individuals become radicalized and take up these calls.

The volume then briefly summarized five examples of terrorism done in the name of faith: ISIL and the conditions under which it has justified brutal acts of violence and murder of tens-of-thousands of civilians; Identity Christianity and the white supremacy movement in the United States; Buddhist monks in Myanmar and their use of faith to justify calls for violence against Muslims; Rabbi Meir Kahane's creation of the Jewish Defense League in the United States and its violence against civilians in the United States and Israel; and Aum Shinrikyo's use of multiple faith traditions to justify attacking Japanese citizens with a chemical weapon in

1995. These cases included some of the most notorious acts of terrorism done in the name of faith and provided a glimpse into the conditions under which religion is weaponized, why groups choose to engage in terrorism, and how these interpretations of the faith persist over time.

Finally, the volume concluded by arguing that countering religiously motivated terrorism requires more than governments adopting a defensive posture, such as homeland security measures aimed at "hardening" potential terrorist targets or imposing emergency measures that may restrict some civil liberties; these measures by themselves do not directly address the underlying causes of religiously motivated terrorism. Similarly, counterterrorism missions executed by law enforcement and militaries aimed at disabling or "decapitating" terrorist organizations are also limited in their ability to address the root causes of religiously motivated terrorism. Ultimately, governments and communities need to work at the local level to address both the factors that make certain individuals and groups vulnerable to embracing calls for violence and terrorism in the name of faith, and to undermine these interpretations of the faith as well. Communities around the world have begun to tackle this problem and provide clues for how best to counter religiously motivated violence, but more work needs to be done.

Bibliography

Afterman, Adam, and Gedaliah Afterman. 2015. "Meir Kahane and Contemporary Jewish Theology of Revenge." *Soundings* 98:2, pp. 192–217.

Aho, James. 1990. *The Politics of Righteousness: Idaho Christian Patriotism*. Seattle: University of Washington Press.

Al-Hadlaq, Abdulrahman. 2011. "Terrorist Rehabilitation: The Saudi Experience." In Rohan Gunaratna, Jolene Jerard, and Lawrence Rubin, eds., *Terrorist Rehabilitation and Counter-Radicalization: New Approaches to Counter-Terrorism*, 59–69. New York: Routledge.

Al-Hitar, Hamoud Abdulhameed. 2011. "Dialogue and Its Effects on Countering Terrorism: The Yemeni Experience." In Rohan Gunaratna, Jolene Jerard, and Lawrence Rubin, eds., *Terrorist Rehabilitation and Counter-Radicalization: New Approaches to Counter-Terrorism*, 109–121. New York: Routledge.

Ali, Mohanad Hage. 2019. "Power Points Defining the Syria-Hizbollah Relationship." *Carnegie Middle East Center*, March 29. https://carnegie-mec.org/2019/03/29/power-points-defining-syria-hezbollah-relationship-pub-78730. Accessed July 14, 2019.

Ali Khan, Liaquat. 2006. "The Essentialist Terrorist." *Washburn Law Journal* 45, pp.47–88.

Aly, Anne, Elizabeth Taylor, and Saul Karnovsky. 2014. "Moral Disengagement and Building Resilience to Violent Extremism: An Education Intervention." *Studies in Conflict and Terrorism* 37:4, pp. 369–385.

Almond, Gabriel A. R., Scott Appleby, and Emanuel Sivan. 2002. *Strong Religion: The Rise of Fundamentalisms around the World*. Chicago: University of Chicago Press.

Amnesty International. 2018. *International Report: 2017/18: The State of the World's Human Rights*. London: Peter Benson House.

Anderton, Charles H., and John R. Carter. 2005. "On Rational Choice Theory and the Study of Terrorism. *Defense and Peace Economics* 16:4, pp. 275–282.

Anti-Defamation League. 2017. "2017 Audit of Anti-Semitic Incidents." www.adl.org/resources/reports/2017-audit-of-anti-semitic-incident s#introduction. Accessed July 15, 2019.

Anti-Defamation League. 2019. "Excerpts of Anti-Defamation League Founding Charter." www.adl.org/who-we-are/excerpt-of-the-anti-defamation-league-founding-charter. Accessed July 17, 2019.

Asad, Talal. 1993. *Genealogies of Religion: Discipline and Reasons of Power in Christianity and Islam*. Baltimore: Johns Hopkins University Press.

Ashour, Omar. 2011. "Islamist Deradicalization in Algeria: The Case of the Islamic Salvation Army and Affiliated Militias." In Rohan Gunaratna, Jolene Jerard, and Lawrence Rubin, eds., *Terrorist Rehabilitation and Counter-Radicalization: New Approaches to Counter-Terrorism*, 11–25. New York: Routledge.

Atran, Scott. 2010. *Talking to the Enemy: Faith, Brotherhood, and the (Un) making of Terrorists*. New York: Ecco.

Axel, Albert, and Hideaki Kase. 2002. *Kamikaze: Japan's Suicide Gods*. London: Pearson Education, 2002.

Barkun, Michael. 1997. *Religion and the Racist Right: The Origins of the Christian Identity Movement*, revised edition. Chapel Hill: University of North Carolina Press.

Barrett, Richard. 2017. "Beyond the Caliphate: Foreign Fighters and the Threat of Returnees." *The Soufan Center*, October 24. https://thesou fancenter.org/research/beyond-caliphate/. Accessed July 15, 2019.

Barron, Laignee. 2017. "Nationalist Monk Known as the Burmese 'bin Laden' Has Been Stopped from Spreading Hate on Facebook." *Time*, February 28. http://time.com/5178790/facebook-removes-wirathu/. Accessed April 23, 2019.

Bayoumy, Yara. 2014. "ISIS Encourages More Attacks on Western 'Disbelievers.'" *Guardian*. September 22. www.independent.co.uk/ news/world/middle-east/isis-urges-more-attacks-on-western-disbelie vers-9749512.html. Accessed January 21, 2019.

Bell, James. 2012. "The World's Muslims: Unity and Diversity." *Pew Forum on Religion and Public Life*. August 9. www.pewforum.org/ 2012/08/09/the-worlds-muslims-unity-and-diversity-executive-sum mary/. Accessed July 15, 2019.

Biardeau, Madeleine. 1989. *Hinduism: The Anthropology of a Civilization*. Translated from French by Richard Nice. Delhi: Oxford University Press.

Bickerman, Elias. 1947. *The Maccabees: An Account of Their History from the Beginnings to the Fall of the House of the Hasmoneans*. Translated by Moses Hadas. New York: Schocken.

Bjørgo, Tore. 2005. "Introduction." In Tore Bojorgo, ed., *Root Causes of Terrorism: Myths, Reality and Ways Forward*, 1–15. New York: Routledge.

Blinder, Alan, and Kevin Sack. 2011. "Dylan Roof Is Sentenced to Death in Charleston Church Massacre." *New York Times*, January 10. www.nytimes .com/2017/01/10/us/dylann-roof-trial-charleston.html. Accessed July 12, 2019.

Bookbinder, Alex. 2013. "969: The Strange Numerological Basis for Burma's Religious Violence." *Atlantic*, April 9. www.theatlantic.com /international/archive/2013/04/969-the-strange-numerological-basis-for-burmas-religious-violence/274816/. Accessed December 10, 2018.

Borum, Randy. 2011. "Radicalization into Violent Extremism: I. A Review of Social Science Theories." *Journal of Strategic Security* 4:4, pp. 7–36.

Boucek, Christopher. 2011. "Extremist Disengagement in Saudi Arabia: Prevention, Rehabilitation and Aftercare." In Rohan Gunaratna, Jolene Jerard, and Lawrence Rubin, eds., *Terrorist Rehabilitation and*

Counter-Radicalization: New Approaches to Counter-Terrorism, 70–90. New York: Routledge.

Brown, Katherine E., and Tania Saeed. 2015. "Radicalisation and Counter-Radicalisation at British Universities: Muslim Encounters and Alternatives." *Ethnic and Racial Studies* 38:11, pp. 1952–1968.

Cambridge English Dictionary. 2019. https://dictionary.cambridge.org/us/dictionary/english. Accessed January 11, 2019.

Campbell, John, and Asch Harwood. 2018. "Boko Haram's Deadly Impact." *Council on Foreign Relations*. August 20. www.cfr.org/article/boko-harams-deadly-impact. Accessed January 21, 2019.

Cavanaugh, William T. 2009. *The Myth of Religious Violence: Secular Ideology and the Roots of Modern Conflict*. New York: Oxford University Press.

Center for Strategic and International Studies. 2018. "Backgrounder: Islamic State Khorasan (IS-K)." www.csis.org/programs/transnational-threats-project/terrorism-backgrounders/islamic-state-khorasan-k. Accessed July 11, 2019.

City of Los Angeles. 2015. "Building Healthy Communities in Los Angeles – Managing Intervention Activities." *Mayor's Office of Public Safety*. www.dhs.gov/sites/default/files/publications/EMW-2016-CA-APP-00294%20Full%20Application.pdf. Accessed July 16, 2019.

Clutterbuck, Lindsay. 2015. "Deradicalization Programs and Counterterrorism: A Perspective on the Challenges and Benefits." *Middle East Institute*, June 10. www.mei.edu/publications/deradicalization-programs-and-counterterrorism-perspective-challenges-and-benefits. Accessed July 16, 2019.

Coclanis, Peter A. 2013. "Terror in Burma: Buddhist vs. Muslims." *World Politics* 176:4, pp. 25–33.

Cohen, Marshall. 2019. "FBI Director Says White Supremacy Is a 'Persistent, Pervasive Threat' to the U.S." *CNN*, April 4. www.cnn.com/2019/04/04/politics/fbi-director-wray-white-supremacy/index.html. Accessed July 15, 2019.

Conze, Edward. 1963. "Buddhist Saviours." In S. G. F. Brandon, ed., *The Saviour God: Comparative Studies in the Concept of Salvation*, 67–82. Manchester: Manchester University Press.

Cook, David. 2007. *Martyrdom in Islam*. New York: Cambridge University Press.

Cordesman, Anthony. 2016. "Terrorism: The Thing We Have to Fear the Most Is Fear Itself." *CSIS*, July 27. www.csis.org/analysis/terrorism-thing-we-have-fear-most-fear-itself. Accessed July 9, 2019.

Crenshaw, Martha. 2006. "The Psychology of Political Terrorism." In M. Hermann, ed., *Political Psychology*, 379–413. San Francisco: Jossey-Bass.

Davis, Danny W. 2010. *The Phinehas Priesthood*. Santa Barbara, CA: Praeger.

Doha Debates. 2019. https://dohadebates.com/. Accessed July 16, 2019.

Dolgin, Janet L. 1977. *Jewish Identity and the JDL*. Princeton: Princeton University Press.

Dorman, Jacob S. 2016. "Dreams Defended and Deferred: The Brooklyn Schools Crisis of 1968 and Black Power's Influence on Rabbi Meir Kahane." *American Jewish History* 100:2, pp. 411–437.

Esposito, John L. 1995. *Islamic Threat: Myth or Reality?* New York: Oxford University Press.

Esposito, John L. 2003. *Oxford Dictionary of Islam*. New York: Oxford University Press.

Fletcher, Jeannine Hill. 2017. *The Sin of White Supremacy: Christianity, Racism and the Religious Diversity of America*. Maryknoll, NY: Orbis.

Fox, Jonathan. 2004. *Ethnoreligious Conflict in the Late Twentieth Century*, Lanham, MD: Lexington Books.

Furnivall, John Sydenham. 1956. *Colonial Policy and Practice: A Comparative Study of Burma and the Netherlands India*. New York: New York University Press.

Gouvernment.fr. 2015. "State of Emergency in France: What Are the Consequences?" www.gouvernement.fr/en/state-of-emergency-in-metropolitan-france-what-are-the-consequences. Accessed July 16, 2019.

Gregg, Heather S. 2010. "Fighting the Jihad of the Pen: Countering Revolutionary Islam's Ideology." *Terrorism and Political Violence* 22:2, pp. 292–314.

Gregg, Heather S. 2014a. "Defining and Distinguishing Traditional and Religious Terrorism." *Perspectives on Terrorism* 8:2, pp. 36–51.

Gregg, Heather S. 2014b. *The Path to Salvation: Religious Violence from the Crusades to Jihad*. Lincoln, NE: Potomac/University of Nebraska Press.

Gregg, Heather S. 2016. "Three Theories of Religious Activism and Violence: Social Movements, Fundamentalists and Apocalyptic War." *Terrorism and Political Violence* 28:2: 338–360.

Gregg, Heather S. 2018. "Religious Resources and Terrorism." *Numen* 65:2–3, pp. 185–206.

Gunaratna, Rohan, and Mohamed Feisal Bin Mohamed Hassan. 2011. "Terrorist Rehabilitation: The Singapore Experience." In Rohan Gunaratna, Jolene Jerard, and Lawrence Rubin, eds., *Terrorist Rehabilitation and Counter-Radicalization: New Approaches to Counter-Terrorism*, 36–58. New York: Routledge.

Hafez, Mohammad, and Creighton Mullins. 2015. "The Radicalization Puzzle: A Theoretical Synthesis of Empirical Approaches to Homegrown Extremism." *Studies in Conflict and Terrorism* 38:11, pp. 958–979.

Hamid, Abul Ghafur. 2016. "Forward." In Melissa Crouch, ed., *Islam and the State in Myanmar: Muslim-Buddhist Relations and the Politics of Belonging*, vii–ix. New York: Oxford University Press.

Haykel, Bernard. 2015. "The History and Ideology of the Islamic State." In Nicholas Burns and Jonathan Price, eds., *Blind Spot: America's Response to the Middle East*, 21–30. Aspen: Aspen Institute.

Hoffman, Bruce. 1998. *Inside Terrorism*. New York: Columbia University Press.

Horgan, John. 2009. *Walking Away from Terrorism: Accounts of Disengagement from Racial and Extremist Movements*. New York: Routledge.

H.R. 3162. 2001. "The U.S.A. Patriot Act." www.congress.gov/bill/107th-congress/house-bill/3162/text/enr, Accessed July 16, 2019.

Huish, Robert, and Patrick Balazo. 2018. "Unliked: How Facebook Is Playing a Role in the Rohingya Genocide." *The Conversation*, January 2. https://theconversation.com/unliked-how-facebook-is-playing-a-part-in-the-rohingya-genocide-89523. Accessed April 23, 2019.

Iannaconne, Lawrence. 1992. "Sacrifice and Stigma: Reducing Free-Riding in Cults, Communes an Other Collectives." *Journal of Political Economy* 100:2, pp. 271–291.

International Crisis Group. 2017. "Buddhist and State Power in Myanmar." *Asia Report No. 290*, September 5. www.crisisgroup.org/asia/south-east-asia/myanmar/290-buddhism-and-state-power-myanmar. Accessed April 23, 2019.

Isakhan, Benjamin, and Jose Antonio Gonzalez Zarandona. 2017. "Layers of Religious and Political Iconoclasm under the Islamic State: Symbolic Sectarianism and Pre-Monotheistic Iconoclasm." *International Journal of Heritage Studies* 24:1, pp. 1–16.

Jones, Seth G. 2018. "The Rise of Far Right Extremism in the United States." *CSIS Briefs*, November 7. www.csis.org/analysis/rise-far-right-extremism-united-states. Accessed May 16, 2019.

Juergensmeyer, Mark. 1992. "Sacrifice and Cosmic War." In Mark Juergensmeyer, ed., *Violence and the Sacred in the Modern World*, 101–117. London: Frank Cass.

Juergensmeyer, Mark. 1993. *The New Cold War? Religious Nationalism Confronts the Secular State*. Berkeley: University of California Press.

Juergensmeyer, Mark. 2000. *Terror in the Mind of God: The Global Rise of Religious Rebellion*. Berkeley: University of California Press.

Juergensmeyer, Mark, and Margo Kitts. 2011. *Princeton Readings in Religion and Violence*. Princeton: Princeton University Press.

Kahane, Meir. 1975. *The Story of the Jewish Defense League*. Radnor, PA: Chilton Book Company.

Kilcullen, David. 2009. *Accidental Guerilla: Fighting Small Wars in the Midst of a Big One*. New York: Oxford University Press.

Kilcullen, David. 2016. *Blood Year: The Unraveling of Western Counterterrorism*. New York: Oxford University Press.

Knight, George R. 1993. *Millennial Fever and the End of the World: A Study of Millerite Adventism*. Boise: Pacific Press.

Kyaw, Nyi Nyi. 2016. "Islamophobia in Buddhist Myanmar: The 969 Movement and Anti-Muslim Violence." In Melissa Crouch, ed., *Islam and the State in Myanmar: Muslim-Buddhist Relations and the Politics of Belonging*, 183–210. New York: Oxford University Press.

Kydd, Andrew, and Barbara Walter. 2006. "Strategies of Terrorism." *International Security* 31:1, pp. 49–80.

Laqueur, Walter. 1987. *The Age of Terrorism*. Boston: Little, Brown and Company.

Laqueur, Walter. 1999. *The New Terrorism: Fanaticism and the Arms of Mass Destruction*. New York: Oxford University Press.

Lenz, Ryan. 2016. "Life after Hate." *The Intelligence Report*, February 14. www.splcenter.org/fighting-hate/intelligence-report/2016/life-after-hate. Accessed July 16, 2019.

Lifton, Robert Jay. 2000. *Destroying the World to Save It: Aum Shinrikyo, Apocalyptic Violence, and the New Global Terrorism*. New York: MacMillian.

Maaga, Mary McCormick. 1998. *Hearing the Voices of Jonestown*. Syracuse: University of Syracuse Press.

Marty, Martin E., and R. Scott Appleby. 1995. "Introduction." In Martin E. Marty and R. Scott Appleby, eds., *Fundamentalisms Comprehended*, 1–10. Chicago: University of Chicago Press.

McCann, Joseph T. 2006. *Terrorism on American Soil*. Boulder: Sentient Publications.

McCants, William. 2015. *The ISIS Apocalypse: The History, Strategy and Doomsday Vision of the Islamic State*. New York: Macmillan.

McCauley, Clark, and Sophia Moskalenko. 2008. "Mechanisms of Political Radicalization: Pathways towards Terrorism." *Studies in Conflict and Terrorism* 20:3, pp. 415–433.

McCauley, Clark, and Sophia Moskalenko. 2017. "Understanding Political Radicalization: The Two Pyramid Model." *American Psychologist* 72:3, pp. 205–216.

Mergui, Raphael, and Phillip Simonnot. 1987. *Israel's Ayatollahs: Meir Kahane and the Far Right in Israel*. London: Saqi Books.

Moghaddam, Fathali. 2005. "The Staircase to Terrorism." *American Psychologist* 60:2, pp. 161–169.

MPAC. 2015. "Safe Spaces: An Updated Toolkit for Empowering Communities And Addressing Ideological Violence." *Muslim Political Action Committee*. www.mpac.org/safespaces/files/MPAC-Safe-Spaces.pdf. Accessed July 16, 2019.

NATO. 2017. "AAP-06 Glossary of Terms and Definitions." North Atlantic Treaty Organization Standardization Office. https://edstar.eda.europa.eu/Standards/Details/03034e98-2a48-4e43-a986-02d0fdbcfa51. Accessed July 18, 2019.

Neumann, Peter R. 2013. "The Trouble with Radicalization." *International Affairs* 89:4, pp. 873–893.

Nobel, Kerry. 2011. *Tabernacle of Hate: Seduction into Right Wing Extremism*, 2nd edition. Syracuse: Syracuse University Press.

Olson, Kyle B. 1999. "Aum Shinrikyo: Once and Future Threat?" *Emerging Infections Diseases* 5:4, pp. 513–516.

Oxford English Dictionary Online. 2019. https://en.oxforddictionaries.com/ Accessed January 4, 2019.

Parachini, John. 2005. "Aum Shinrikyo." In Brian Jenkins, ed., *Aptitude for Destruction: Case Studies of Organizational Learning in Five Terrorist Groups*, volume 5, 11–35. Santa Monica: RAND.

Pedahzur, Ami, and Arie Perliger. 2009. *Terrorism in Israel*. New York: Columbia University Press.

Peri, Yoram. 2013. "Kahane, Meir 1932–1990." In Patrick L. Mason, ed., *Encyclopedia of Race and Racism*. New York: Macmillan.

Perliger, Ari. 2012. "Challengers from the Sidelines: Understanding America's Violent Far Right." *Countering Terrorism Center at West Point*, November. https://ctc.usma.edu/challengers-from-the-sidelines-under standing-americas-violent-far-right/. Accessed May 16, 2019.

QIASS. 2012. "Countering Violent Extremism: Community Engagement Programmes in Europe." *Qatar International Academy for Security Studies*. www.soufangroup.com/wp-content/uploads/2013/12/ QIASS-CVE-Paper-Phase-II-Paper-I.pdf. Accessed July 16, 2019.

Quilliam Foundation. 2019. www.quilliaminternational.com/. Accessed July 16, 2019.

Ranstorp, Magnus. 1997. *Hizb'allah in Lebanon: The Politics of Western Hostage Crisis*. New York: St. Martin's Press.

Rapoport, David C. 1983. "Fear and Trembling: Terrorism in Three Religious Traditions." *American Political Science Review* 78:3, pp. 658–677.

Rapoport, David C. 2004. "The Four Waves of Modern Terrorism." In A. K. Cronin and J. M. Ludes, eds., *Attacking Terrorism: Elements of a Grand Strategy*, 46–73. Washington, DC: Georgetown University Press.

Rapoport, David C. 1999. "Terrorism and the Weapons of the Apocalypse." *National Security Studies Quarterly* 5:3, pp. 49–63.

Reader, Ian. 1996. *A Poisonous Cocktail? Aum Shinrikyo's Path to Violence*. Copenhagen, Denmark: Nordic Institute of Asian Studies.

Richardson, Louise. 2006. *What Terrorists Want: Understanding the Enemy, Containing the Threat*. New York: Random House.

Robins, Robert S., and Jerrold M. Post. 1997. *Political Paranoia: The Psychopolitics of Hatred*. New Haven: Yale University Press.

Rubin, Lawrence. 2011. "Non-Kinetic Approaches to Counter-Terrorism: A Case Study of Egypt and the Islamic Jihad." In Rohan Gunaratna, Jolene Jerard, and Lawrence Rubin, eds., *Terrorist Rehabilitation and Counter-Radicalization: New Approaches to Counter-Terrorism*, 26–35. New York: Routledge.

Saslow, Eli. 2018. *Rising Out of Hatred: The Awakening of a White Nationalist*. New York: Random House.

Serwer, Adam. 2019. "White Nationalism's Deep American Roots." *Atlantic*, April. www.theatlantic.com/magazine/archive/2019/04/adam-serwer-madison-grant-white-nationalism/583258/. Accessed August 17, 2019.

Sharpe, Tanya Telfair. 2000. "The Identity Christian Movement: Ideology of Domestic Terrorism." *Journal of Black Studies* 30:4, pp. 604–623.

Sick, Gary G. 1990. "The Political Underpinnings of Terrorism." In Charles W. Kegley, Jr., ed., *International Terrorism: Characteristics, Causes Controls*, 52–54. London: Palgrave.

Simons, Erica. 2006. "Faith, Fanaticism and Fear: Aum Shinrikyo – The Birth and Death of a Terrorist Organization." *Forensic Examiner* 15:1, pp. 37–45.

Smart, Ninian. 1996. *Dimensions of the Sacred: An Anatomy of the World's Beliefs*. Berkeley: University of California Press.

Smith, Christian. 1996. "Introduction: Correcting a Curious Neglect, or Bringing Religion Back in." In Christian Smith, ed., *Disruptive Religion:*

The Force of Faith in Social Movement Activism, 1–28. New York: Routledge.

Southern Poverty Law Center. 2019a. "Alt-Right." www.splcenter.org/fight ing-hate/extremist-files/ideology/alt-right. Accessed July 15, 2019.

Southern Poverty Law Center. 2019b. "The Jewish Defense League." www.splcenter.org/fighting-hate/extremist-files/group/jewish-defense-league. Accessed May 5, 2019.

Spiro, Melford E. 1982. *Buddhism and Society: A Great Tradition and Its Burmese Vicissitudes*, 2nd edition. Berkeley: University of California Press.

Sprinzak, Ehud, 1992. "Violence and Catastrophe in the Theology of Rabbi Meir Kahane: The Idealization of Mimetic Desire." In Mark Juergensmeyer, ed., *Violence and the Sacred in the Modern World*, 48–70. London: Frank Cass.

Stone, Douglas M. 2011. "Thinking Strategically about Terrorist Rehabilitation: Lessons from Iraq." In Rohan Gunaratna, Jolene Jerard, and Lawrence Rubin, eds., *Terrorist Rehabilitation and Counter-Radicalization: New Approaches to Counter-Terrorism*, 91–109. New York: Routledge.

Straits Times. 2018. "Philippine Military New Leader of ISIS in South East Asia." March 6. www.straitstimes.com/asia/se-asia/philippine-military-identifies-new-leader-of-isis-in-south-east-asia. Accessed January 21, 2019.

Sude, Barbara, David Stebbins, and Sarah Weilant. 2015. "Lessening the Risk of Refugee Radicalization: Lessons for the Middle East from Past Crises." *RAND Perspective*. www.rand.org/content/dam/rand/pubs/perspectives/PE100/PE166/RAND_PE166.pdf. Accessed July 16, 2019.

Sullivan, Colleen. 2011. "Aum Shinrikyo." In Gus Martin, ed., *The Sage Encyclopedia of Terrorism*, 1–4. Thousand Oaks, CA: Sage Publications.

Syan, Hardip Singh. 2012. *Sikh Militancy in the Seventeenth Century: Religious Violence in Mughal and Early Indian History*. London: I. B. Tauris.

Tan, Vivian. 2017. "More than 168,000 Rohingya Likely Fled Myanmar Since 2012 – UNHCR Report." *United Nations High Commission for Refugees.* www.unhcr.org/en-us/news/latest/2017/5/590990ff4/168000-rohingya-likely-fled-myanmar-since-2012-unhcr-report.html. Accessed May 31, 2019.

Torok, Thomas J. et al. 1997. "A Large Community Outbreak of Salmonellosis Caused by Intentional Contamination of Restaurant Salad Bars." *Journal of the American Medical Association* 278:5, pp. 389–395.

United Nations. 2018. "Unearthing Atrocities: Mass Graves in Territory Formerly Controlled by ISIL." *UN Assistance Mission for Iraq and United Nations Office of the High Commissioner for Human Rights.* www.uniraq.com/index.php?searchword=mass%20grave&categories=190,110,156,159,115,158,154,161,164,172,162,163,173,155,170&option=com_k2&view=itemlist&task=search&lang=en. Accessed January 14, 2019.

UN News. 2017. "UN Human Rights Chief Points to 'Textbook Example of Ethnic Cleansing' in Myanmar." September 11. https://news.un.org/en/story/2017/09/564622-un-human-rights-chief-points-textbook-example-ethnic-cleansing-myanmar. Accessed April 23, 2019.

US Federal Bureau of Investigation. 2018. "Terrorism." www.fbi.gov/investigate/terrorism. Accessed July 17, 2019.

Vatican Press Office. 2018. "Presentazione dell'Annuario Pontificio 2018 e dell' 'Annuarium Statisticum Ecclesiae' 2016," June 13. https://press.vatican.va/content/salastampa/it/bollettino/pubblico/2018/06/13/0440/00957.html. Accessed July 15, 2019.

Vidino, Lorenzo. 2008. "A Preliminary Assessment of Counter-Radicalization in the Netherlands." *Counter Terrorism Center Sentinel* 1:9, pp. 12–13.

Walsh, Declan, and Nour Yussef. 2017. "Militants Kill 305 at Sufi Mosque in Egypt's Deadliest Terror Attack." *New York Times*, November 24. www.nytimes.com/2017/11/24/world/middleeast/mosque-attack-egypt.html. Accessed January 14, 2019.

Washington Post. 2001. "'Oh God, Open All Doors for Me.'" *Washington Post*, September 28, www.washingtonpost.com/archive/politics/2001/09/28/oh-god-open-all-doors-for-me/c9801ab1-3c9e-49df-9928-9df002c549ba/?utm_term=.6e559b5e7d97. Accessed November 23, 2018.

Weber, Max. 1963. *The Sociology of Religion*, translated by Ephraim Fischoff. Boston: Beacon Press.

Wictorowicz, Quintan. 2006. "Anatomy of the Salafi Movement." *Studies in Conflict and Terrorism* 29:3, pp. 207–239.

Wictorowicz, Quintan. 2005. *Radical Islam Rising: Muslim Extremism in the West*. Lanham, MD: Rowman & Littlefield.

Williams, Brian Glyn. 2016. *Counter Jihad: America's Military Experience in Afghanistan, Iraq and Syria*. Philadelphia: University of Pennsylvania Press.

Wood, Graeme. 2015. "What ISIS Really Wants." *Atlantic*, March 15. www.theatlantic.com/magazine/archive/2015/03/what-isis-really-wants/384980/. Accessed August 25, 2018.

Wright, Stuart. A. 2011. "Revisiting the Branch Davidian Mass Suicide Debate." In James R. Lewis, *Violence and New Religious Movements*, 113–132. New York: Oxford University Press.

Yegar, Moshe. 2002. *Between Integration and Secession: The Muslim Communities of the Southern Philippines, Southern Thailand, and Western Burma/Myanmar*. Lanham, MD: Lexington Books.

Yegar, Moshe. 1972. *The Muslims of Burma: A Study of a Minority Group*, Schriftenreihe Des Südasien-Instituts Der Universität Heidelberg. Wiesbaden, Germany: Otto Harrassowitz.

Young, Reuven. 2006. "Defining Terrorism: The Evolution of Terrorism as a Legal Concept in International Law and its Influence on Definitions in Domestic Legislation." *Boston College International and Comparative Law Review* 29:1, pp. 23–103.

Zin, Min. 2015. "Anti-Muslim Violence in Burma: Why Now?" *Social Research* 82:2, pp. 375–398.

Cambridge Elements ≡

Religion and Violence

James R. Lewis
University of Tromsø

James R. Lewis is Professor of Religious Studies at the
University of Tromsø, Norway and the author and editor of
a number of volumes, including *The Cambridge Companion to
Religion and Terrorism.*

Margo Kitts
Hawai'i Pacific University

Margo Kitts edits the *Journal of Religion and Violence* and is
Professor and Coordinator of Religious Studies and East-West
Classical Studies at Hawai'i Pacific University in Honolulu.

ABOUT THE SERIES

Violence motivated by religious beliefs has become all too common
in the years since the 9/11 attacks. Not surprisingly, interest in the
topic of religion and violence has grown substantially since then.
This Elements series on Religion and Violence addresses this new,
frontier topic in a series of c. fifty individual Elements. Collectively,
the volumes will examine a range of topics, including violence in
major world religious traditions, theories of religion and violence,
holy war, witch hunting, and human sacrifice, among others.

Cambridge Elements ☰

Religion and Violence

Printed in the United States
By Bookmasters